Matthews's new Bristol Directory, for the
Year, 1793-4.

MATTHEWS's
NEW
BRISTOL DIRECTORY,
For the YEAR, 1793-4.

CONTAINING AN

ALPHABETICAL LIST

OF THE

CORPORATION, CLERGY, MERCHANTS, BANKERS,
PROFFESSORS OF THE LAW AND PHYSIC,
MANUFACTURERS, PRINCIPAL
TRADERS, &c. &c.

OF THE CITY OF

B R I S T O L,

WITH ITS ENVIRONS.

TO WHICH ARE ADDED

LISTS of the MAIL COACHES, WAGGONS, COASTING
and other TRADING VESSELS,

TO AND FROM BRISTOL.

PARTICULARS OF THE

COMING IN and GOING OUT of the POSTS, *Home* and *Foreign*;

WITH THE

CUSTOM-HOUSE, EXCISE-OFFICE, &c.

ALSO

A LIST of the HACKNEY COACHES, with their Owners.

B R I S T O L;

Printed and Sold by WILLIAM MATTHEWS, No. 10, BROAD
MEAD, and may be had of the Bookfellers in Town and Country.

BRISTOL DIRECTORY.

CORPORATION of BRISTOL.

MAYOR.
Henry Bengough Efq.
Richard Burke, Efq Recorder.

ALDERMEN.
Thomas Deane, Efq.
Thomas Harris, Efq.
Sir John Durbin, Knt
William Miles, Efq.
Edward Brice, Efq.
John Anderfon, Efq.
John Farr, Efq.
George Daubeny, Efq.
Levi Ames, Efq.
John Harris, Efq.
John Noble, Efq.

LATE MAYORS.
Henry Cruger, Efq.
John Crofts, Efq.
James Hill, Efq.

SHERIFFS.
William Gibbons, Efq.
Jofeph Gregory Harris, Efq.

COMMON COUNCIL.
Sir James Laroche, Bart.
Matthew Brickdale, Efq.
Jeremy Baker, Efq.
John Fifher Weare, Efq.
Benjamin Lofcombe, Efq.

James Morgan, Efq.
Jofeph Harford, Efq.
Samuel Span, Efq.
Jofeph Smith, Efq
Robert Coleman, Efq.
Rowland Williams, Efq.
William Weare, Efq.
James Harvev, Efq.
Richard Bright, Efq.
Evan Bailie, Efq.
Thomas Daniel, jun. Efq.
John Morgan, Efq.
Robert Claxton, Efq.
Philip Protheroe, Efa.
John Gordon, jun Efq.
Charles Young, Efq.
Richard Blake, Efq.
John Page, Efq.
R. Hawkefwell, Efq. *Chamberlain*.
Sam. Worrall, jun. Efq. *Town-clk*.
Arthur Palmer, *Under Sheriff*
John Lewis, *Clerk of the Arraigns*.

John Lewis,
G. Merrick, } *Clks to the Town-cl*.

George Webb Hall, *Deputy Regifte, of the Court of Confcience*.

BRISTOL CATHEDRAL.

Dr Spencer Madan, Bifhop of Briftol, *refides partly at London and partly at Briftol Palace*.

Dr. John Hallem, Dean; *half the year at Windfor, and half a year at Briftol Deanry*.

A 2

Edmund

Edmund Gibfon, Chancellor, re-
fides in Bifhop-Storford, Herts.
Rev Geo. Watfon Hand, A. M
Archdeacon, refides at London
Rev. John Cox. Preb. Margaret-
ftreet, Cavendifh fquare, London.
Rev. Tho. Powys, Prebendary.
Fauly near He.ley, Oxfordfhire.
Rev. F. W. Blomberg, Preben-
dary, Briftol.
Rev. Dr. Chapman. Preb. Bath.
Rev. F. Randolph, Preb. Ditto.

Rev. Dr J. Whateiv, Preb Sarm
Rev. Edw. Bowles, Precentor &
Minor-Canon, Lower-green.
Rev, Jas. Brown, Minor-Canor,
Caftle-green.
Rev. B. Wood, Minor-Canon,
Kingsdown.
Rev. John Muttlebury, Minor-
Canon, College-fire t.
George Rogers, Chapter-Clerk,
Lower-green.

CLERGY refident in BRISTOL.

Allen, Rev James, Hotwells
Baker. Rev. Slade, Redland.
Bale, Rev. Mr. Park-row
Biddolph, Rev. Thomas, Cathay
Bull, Rev. John, Redcrofs-ftreet
Camplin, Rev. John, Lower-green.
Camplin, Rev. Wm. North-ftreet
Cafberd, Rev John, Lower-green.
Cafberd, Rev. Dr. College-green
Collinfon, Rev. Rich. Park-ftreet
Cooke, Rev. Mr. Lodge-ftreet.
Criche, Rev. P. S. Temple-ftreet
Davies, Rev. R. Durdham-down
Deake, Rev. John, College-ftreet.
Edwards, Rev. W. E Redland
Ford, Rev. Dr. John, Clifton.
Gravenor, Rev. L. Upper Maud-l
Greville, Rev. Mr. St. Michaels-b
Harding, Rev. Rich. Berkely-fq
Hicks, Rev. Geo. Queen-fquare
Holder, Rev. H. E. Paul-ftreet.
Horndon Rev. Mr. St Jas's ch-yd.
Hutchefon, Rev. Mr. St James' fq.
Johnes, Rev. Thomas, City Li-
brarian, King-ftreet.
Lee, Rev. Charles, Unity-ftreet
New, Rev, James, Redcrofs-ftreet.
Pidding, Rev. Jas. Montague-ftr
Rimbron, Rev Mr St. Michaels b.
Robins, Rev. Dr. Guinea-ftreet
Seyer, Rev Sam Royal Fort
Sheppard, Rev. E. Clifton-hill
Shipton, Rev John, King-fquare.
Sims, Rev. Mr. Queens-parade.
Small, Rev. J. A. D. D. Portl fq.
Spike, Rev Dr. Lower-green.
Spry, Rev. B. A. M. Redcliff-hill
Stonehoufe, Rev. Mr. Hotwell-pa.
Tucker, Rev. Dr. Dean of Glo-
cefter, Queen-fquare.
Wait, Rev. Wm. King-fquare
Walcam, Rev. Jofeph, Park.
Watfon, Rev. Sam. Temple-backs.
Watfon, Rev. Rob. Bedminfter.
Wilkins, Rev. Geo. Church-lane
Wilmot, Rev. R. St. James's-fq.
Wilfon, Rev. William, Clifton.
Wood, Rev. Mr. Kingsdown-par.

DISSENTING CLERGY.

Bradburn, Rev. Sam. Southwell-ft.
Bryant, Rev. Rob. Duke-ftreet.
Davies, Rev. Jas. Upper Maud.-la.
De Soyres, Francis, Park.
Efton, Rev. J. P. St. Michaels-b
Hartley, Rev. John, Black-friers
Hey, Rev. John, Dove-ftreet.
Hughes, Rev Mr. Ditto.
Plowden, Rev. Rob. Prieft to the
Romifh Chapel, Trenchard-la.
Thomas, Rev. Mr. Cumberland-ft.
Wright, Rev. John, Barton.

PHYSIC.

P H Y S I C.

Allard, R. T. *Surgeon*, Unity-ftreet
Barry, Richard, *Apothecary*, Dowry-fquare.
Baylis, Edward, *M D* Jacob's-well.
Baynton, Thomas, *Surgeon*, Old-market.
Burjew, John Pine, *Apothecary*, High-ftreet
Blagden and Dew, *Apothecaries*, Barton
Bowles, Francis, *Surgeon*, College-ftreet.
Brickendon, Thomas, *Surgeon*, Lodge-ftreet.
Bumble, John, *Druggift*, Weft-ftreet
Calder and Batt, *Apothecaries* Dowry-fquare
Caftleman, John, *Surgeon*, Dighton-ftreet
Cave, John and Co *Druggifts*, Redcliff-ftreet.
Cornifh, James, *Surgeon*, Great Ann-ftreet
Cox, I M *M D* Unity-ftreet.
Date, James, *Apothecary*, Barton.
Davis, Edward, *Surgeon*, Stokes-croft.
Davis, Ebenezer, *Surgeon*, Kingfdown.
Duck, John, *Apothecary*, Hotwells
Duck, John, *Apothecary*, Caftle-ftreet.
Durbin, Henry, *Chymift*, Redcliff-ftreet.
Dyer, Gold and Dyer, *Apothecaries*, Bridge-ftreet.
Dyer, Robert, *Apothecary*, King-fquare
Edwards, James, *Apothecary*, Broad-ftreet.
Fletcher, John, *M D*. Glocefter-ftreet.
Fox, Edward Long, *M D* Caftle-green.
Fry, John, *Druggift*, Caftle-ftreet.
Godwin and Innes, *Chymifts and Druggifts*, Wine-ftreet.
Goldwyer, William, *Surgeon*, Bridge-ftreet.
Griffiths, Thomas, *Apothecary*, Caftle-green.
Hughes, John, *Apothecary*, Chapel-row, Hotwells
Illing, James, *Druggift and Chymift*, Caftle-ftreet
Jardine, Lewis Jones, *Surgeon*, Manfion-houfe-ftreet.
Johnfon, George Milligen, *M D*. College-green.
Jones, David, *Surgeon*, Broad-mead
Kelfon, James, *Apothecary*, Stokes-croft.
Lawrence, William, *Surgeon and Man Midwife*, Bedminfter.
Lewis, William, *M D*. King-fquare
Lewis, Corfer and Co *Druggifts and Chymifts*, Redcliff-ftreet.
Lovell, Robert, *M D* Berkely-fquare.
Lowe, Godfrey, *Surgeon*, Queen-fquare.
Ludlow, Abraham, *M. D*. Cumberland-ftreet.
Martin, John, *Apothecary*, Quay.
Martin, George, *Apothecary and Man Midwife*, Bedminfter-caufe.

Maurice,

Maurice, Joseph, *Apothecary*, St. Michaels-hill.
Metford, Joseph, *Surgeon*, Wilder-ftreet.
Moncrieffe, Wm. *M. D.* Great George'-ftreet.
Morgan, James and John, *Druggifts*, Corn-ftreet.
Mofs, James, *Apothecary*, Old-market.
Newland, Peter, *Surgeon and Apothecary*, Old-market.
Newman, John, *Surgeon*, Caftle-ftreet.
Noble, John Padmore, *Surgeon*, College-green.
O'Ryan, John, *M. D.* St. Auguftines-place.
Plomer, James, *M. D.* Park-ftreet,
Prieft, Robert, *M. D.* St. Auguftines-back.
Probyn, James, *Surgeon and Apothecary*, Bridge-ftreet.
Pye, James, *Surgeon*, Clifton.
Pye, Thomas, *Surgeon*, Upper Eafton.
Rich, Thomas, *Apothecary*, Broad-mead.
Rufs, John, *Apothecary*, Clifton.
Safford, Joseph, *Surgeon and Apothecary*, Old-market.
Safford, Joseph, *Apothecary*, Redcliff-hill.
Shapland, Joseph, *Apothecary*, Park-ftreet.
Shedden and Co. *Druggifts*, Wine-ftreet.
Shellard, Thomas, *M. D.* Redland,
Shellard, Henry, *Apothecary*, Park-ftreet.
Short, Samuel Henderfon, *Surgeon*, St. Auguftines-place.
Shute, Thomas, *Surgeon*, Park-ftreet.
Simpfou, Robert and Son, *Apothecaries*, Caftle-ftreet.
Southall, Norman, *Apothecary*, North-ftrcet.
Tilladams, Ann, *Druggift*, Union-ftreet.
Townfend, John, *Surgeon*, Broad-ftreet.
Ward, Danvers, *Surgeon*, John-ftreet.
Watts, Mary, *Apothecary*, Caftle-ftreet.
Wells and Arthur, *Druggifts*, Back.
Williams, Samuel, *Apothecary*, Broad-ftreet.
Wilmot, Edward, *Chymift and Druggift*, Thomas-ftreet.
Wright, John, *M. D.* Barton.
Yeatman, Morgan, *Surgeon*, Orchard-ftreet.
Yeatman, Charlton, *Surgeon and Apothecary*, Thomas-ftreet.
Yeo, William, *Apothecary*, Dowry-fquare.

ATTORNEYS AT LAW.

Anderdon, John, *Park-ftreet.*
Bayley, John, *Corn-ftreet.*
Baynton, Daniel, *Old-market.*
Bigg, Robert, *Balduin-ftreet.*
Bird, Fenwick, *St. Jas's ch.-yd.*
Broughton, John, *College-green.*
Bull, Tho. Evans, *Redcrofs-ft.*
Camplin, Chas. *Remfon's-bath.*
Child, George, *Exchange.*
Cninn, Edward, *Stokes-croft.*

Cooke,

Cooke, Isaac, *Corn-street*.
Concannon, Matt. *Jacob-street*
Concannon, Geo. jun. *Bath-street*
Cox, William, *Broad-street*.
Cunningham, Matt. *Small-street*.
Daniel, Edward, *Castle-green*.
Daubeny, Giles, *Clare-street*.
Davis, Henry, *Ditto*.
Drummond, And. Barr. *King-sq.*
Elderton, Harry, *Small-street*.
Fisher, Thomas, *Ditto*.
Grabham, G. L. *Quay*.
Gundry, William. *Redcross-street*
Gundry, James, *Maryport-street*.
Gyles, John, *Old-market*.
Hall, G. W. *All-saints-lane*.
Hawkeswell, Joseph, *Wine-street*.
Hawkins, Matt. *Queen-square*
Hetling, Thomas, *Broad-street*.
Hughes and James, *Corn-street*.
Jacobs, Richard, *Queen-square*.
James, George, *Stokes-croft*.
Jarman, Thomas, *Duke-street*.
Jenkins Richard, *Dowry square*
Jesse, Robert, *Stokes-croft*
Jones, Thomas, *Old-market*.
Lemans, Messrs *Wine-street*.
Lewis, John, Attorney at Council-house, *Lower-green*.
Martin, George, *High-street*
Mengrove, Tho. *Old-market*.
Merrick, George, *Milk-street*.
Miller, *Bridge-street*
Morgan, Thomas, *Bridge-street*.

Morgan and Coates, *Small street*.
Morle, William *Bridge-street*.
Morrow, Robert *Thomas-street*.
Osborne and Seager, *Broad-st*.
Parkers and Clarke, *John-street*.
Patten, James, *Barton-hill*.
Payne, Robert, *John-street*.
Pember, Richard, *Union-street*, Attorney and Solicitor, Master in Chancery, Notary Public, a Commissioner for taking and receiving of Affidavits, in the several Courts of Kings Bench, Common Pleas Exchequer, & Duchy Court of Lancaster.
Perry, William, *Small-street*.
Pullen, James, *Redcliff-street*.
Raekster, William *Exchange*.
Shering, G. D. *Unity-st. St. Phps*
Simmons, Samuel, *John-street*.
Stokes, Thomas, *Castle-street*.
Strickland, G. *St Augustines-back*.
Syme, Joseph, *St Stephen-street*.
Symons, Thomas, *All-saints-lane*.
Usher, John, *Cumberland-street*.
Ward, Francis *Exchange*
Way, Tho *Taylors-court, Broad-st*.
Weaver, Tho. *King-square avenue*.
Weeks, James, *Corn-street*.
Williams, John, *Exchange*.
Windey and James, *Corn-street*.
Woodford, R D. *Clare-street*.
Woodward, J N. *Orchard-street*.

BANKING COMPANIES.

Ames, Cave, Harford, Dauheny, and Bright, *Corn-street*; draw on Down, Thornton, and Free, 1, *Bartbelomew lane, London*.

Davis, Henry and Sons, *Small-street*, draw on Forster, Lubbock, Bosanquet and Co. 11, *Mansion-house street, London*.

Deane, Whitehead, and Co. *Small-street*; draw on John and George Whitehead, 5, *Basinghall-street, London*.

Harris and Savery, *Narrow Wine-street*; draw on Sir James Esdaile, Knt. Esdaile, Hammet, and Esdaile, 73, *Lombard-st London*.

Tyndal,

Tyrdal, Elton, and Co. *Corn-street;* draw on Prescott, Grote Culverden, and Hollingworth, 62, *Threadneedle-street, London.*

Vaughans, Baker, and Co. *Corn-street;* (shut at 12 Fridays) draw on Barnet, Hoare, Hill, and Barnet, 62, *Lombard-street, London.*

Wigan, Thomas, *Bridge-street;* draws on Goodbehere, Wigan and Co. *London.*

Worrall and Blatchley, *Exchange;* draw on Baron Dimsdale Sons, Barnard and Sons, 50, *Cornhill, London.*

MERCHANTS, TRADERS, &c.

ABBOTT, Thomas, *Custom-house officer,* Southwell-street

Abbott, Joseph, *Taylor,* Thomas-street.

Acraman, William, *Merchant,* Princes-street.

Acraman, William and Son, *Ship-chandlers,* Ditto.

Adams, John, *Tyler and Plaisterer,* York-street.

Adams, John, *Black Boy,* Princes-street.

Adams, Thomas, *Pastry-cook and Confectioner,* Castle-street.

Adams, Samuel, *Confectioner,* Bedminster.

Adams, William, *Straggler,* Quay.

Adamson, Capt. Robert, College-street.

Adamson, James, *Accomptant,* Elbroad-street.

Addis, John, *Old Kings-head,* Passage-street, St. Phillips.

Addison, Hester, *Stationer,* Bridewell-lane.

Addison, Hester, *Stationer,* Quay-street.

Adlam, Thomas, *Accomptant,* Jamaica-street.

Adlam, William, *Accomptant,* Redcross-street.

Adlam, James, *Hair-dresser,* Back-street.

Ady, William, *Accomptant,* Stokes-croft.

Albrook, Thomas, *Smith,* Bedminster.

Alden, John, *Butcher,* West-street.

Alden, James, *Butcher,* Butcher-row.

Alderwick, Mary, *Fountain,* Queen-street.

Aldridge, Richard, Esq. *Banker,* Queen-square.

Aldridge, Mr. Thomas, 3, Somerset-square.

Aldridge, Richard, *Sail-cloth and Twine-maker,* Quay

Aldwin, *Lodging-house,* St. Vincents-parade, Hotwells.

Allen, Frances, *Dealer in Spirits,* Quay.

Allen, Anthony, *Carpenter,* Hotwell-road.

Allen, Mrs. Catharine, 26, Trinity-street.

Allen, Mrs. F. Orchard-street.

Allen, James, *Mariner,* Lower Maudlin-lane.

Allen, John, *Hat-manufacturer,* Christmas-street.

Allen, Joseph, *Ironmonger,* West-street.

Allen

Allen, Joseph, *Accomptant*, Lawrence-hill.
Allen, Robert, *Cabinet-maker*, Back-street.
Allen, James, *Architect*, Thomas-street.
Allen, John, Gent. 3. Cathay.
Alexander, John, *Broker and Auctioneer*, Broad-mead.
Alman, Aaron *Silversmith*, Glocester-lane.
Alman, Joseph, *Pawnbroker*, Thomas-street.
Alman, Isaac, *Watch-maker and Jeweller*, Bedminster-causeway.
Allport, John, *Smith and Farrier*, Leek-lane.
Allport, John, *Seven Stars*, Callowhill-street.
Alsop, James, *Brown Stone Potter*, Temple-street.
Ambrose, M'Carthy and Co. *Grocers and Tobacconists*, Back.
Ames, Hellicar and Sons, *Merchants*, Queen-square.
Ames, Cave, Harford, Daubeny and Bright, *Bankers*, Corn-street.
Ames, Richard, *Lodging-house*, 6, Granby-place, Hotwells.
Ames, Levi, Esq. Clifton.
Ames and Williams, *Dry-salters*, Castle-green.
Amos and Cox, *Woollen-drapers and Salesmen*, Union-street.
Amos, Isaac, Gent. 20, College-green.
Ancran, Michael, *Accomptant*, Clifton.
Anderson, John, *Merchant*, Princes-street.
Anderson, James, *Dealer in Horses*, Charles-street.
Anderson, John, Esq. *Alderman*, Durdham-down.
Andrass and Co. *Foreign and British Toy-warehouse*, Clare-street.
Andrass, Mrs. Frances, Upper Maudlin-lane.
Andrews, Thomas *Three Crowns*, Old King-street.
Andrews, Jesse, Gent. St. Michaels-hill.
Andrews, John, *Tyler and Plaisterer*, Charles-street.
Andrews, Thomas, Esq. Duke-street.
Andrews, Joan, *Jolly Skinner*, Wade-street.
Andrews, William, *Pawnbroker*, Three Queen-lane.
Angel, William, *Leg and Crown*, Bear-lane.
Anion, John, *Carver and Gilder*, Bell, Broad-mead.
Anstice, Mary, *Dealer in Spirits*, Ditto.
Anthony, John, *Sadler and Bridle-cutter*, Ditto.
Antrobus, John, *Mariner*, Lower-green
Antrobus, John, *Clog-maker*, Upper Maudlin-lane.
Apperley, Thomas, *Mayor's-officer*, St. James's church-yard.
Appleby, William, *Butcher*, Butcher-row.
Archer, William, *Baker*, North-street.
Arden, Francis, *Butcher*, Broad Ware.
Ariel, William, Gent. St. Augustines-back.
Armitage, William, *Teacher of the Mathematics*, St. Augustines-place.
Arnold, John, *Excise Export-officer*, Somerset-place.

B

Arnold,

Arnold, Robert, *Book-keeper*, Thomas-ftreet.
Arnold, George, *Gardener*, Pennywell-lane.
Arnold, Ellen, *Midwife*, Newgate-ftreet.
Arnold, Mary, *Swan Inn*, Stokes-croft.
Arnold, John, *Undertaker*, Bridge-ftreet.
Arfcott, William, *Prince Royal Ship*, Griffin-lane.
Arthur, Mrs. Ann, 37, Queen-fquare.
Arundel, Thomas, *Smith, and Screw-maker*, Bear-lane.
Afelby, Capt. John, College-ftreet.
Afelby, Mifs   Short-grove, Durdham-down.
Afh, Samuel, *Linen-draper*, Newfoundland-ftreet.
Afh, Mr. Edward, 18, King-fquare.
Afh, Mr. Gregory, 19, Ditto.
Afh, Mrs. Hefter, 14, St. James's-fquare.
Afh, Edward, *Raifin Wine-maker, &c.* Temple-ftreet.
Afhburner John, *Livery Stable-keeper*, Duck-lane.
Afhbury, William, *Umbrella-maker*, Hope-fquare, Hotwells.
Afhford, Elizabeth, *Nag's Head*, King-ftreet.
Afkins, Mrs. Ann, Redcliff-hill.
Afhley, Robert, *Tyler and Plaifterer*, Charlotte-ftreet.
Afhley, William, *Butcher*, St. James's-back.
Afhman, Elizabeth, *Hair-dreffer*, John-ftreet.
Afton, Matthew, *Plumber*, Redcliff-ftreet.
Atkins, Henry, *Wine-merchant*, Back.
Atkins, William, *Taylor*, Broad-mead.
Atwood, Rofe, *Poulterer*, Hotwell-road.
Atwood, Jacob William, *Hooper*, Dove-ftreet.
Atwood, Mrs. Sarah, 7, Somerfet-fquare.
Auftin, Sarah, *School-miftrefs*, Cathay.
Auftin, Aaron, *Brick-maker*, Eugean-ftreet, St Philip's.
Auftin, Aaron, *Smith and Farrier*, Old-market.
Auftin, Aaron, *Clock and Vice-maker*, Ditto.
Avard, Sampfon, *Carpenter*, Milk-ftreet.
Avard, Jofeph, *Watch-maker*, Union-ftreet.
Avery, Richard, *Lodging-houfe*, King-ftreet.

B

Babb, Capt. William, 15, Princes-ftreet
Babb, Thomas, *Mate of a Ship*, 14, Pipe-lane.
Baber, Henry, *Sheriff's-officer*, Bedminfter.
Bachelor, Thomas, *Silk-mercer*, Bridge-ftreet.
Badham, Richard, *Cabinet-maker*, Boot-lane, Bedminfter.
Bailey, Mrs. *Lodging-houfe*, Manfion-houfe-ftreet.

Bailey,

Bailey, George, *Peruke-maker*, Maryport-street.
Bailey, Capt. John, College-street.
Bailey, Mr. William, Trinity-street.
Bailey, Evan, Esq. Park-row.
Bailey, William, *Carver*, Stoney-hill.
Bailey, James, *Cabinet-maker*, Horfield-road.
Bailey, John, *Baker*, Narrow Wine-street.
Bailey, George, *Merchant*, Castle-green.
Bailey, Bettington, and Co. *Lead-merchants*, Ditto.
Bailey, Dean, Gent. 5, Redcross-street,
Bailey, Henry, *Stocking-manufacturer*, West-street.
Bailey, Thomas, *Fruiterer*, 32, Redcliff-street.
Bailey, Mr John, Bread-street, St. Philips.
Baker, Isaac, *Hat-maker*, Milk-street.
Baker, John, *Kings Arms*, Ditto.
Baker, Sarah, *Milliner and Mantua-maker*, Ditto.
Baker, Samuel, *Bell*, Old King-street,
Baker, William, *Oyster-merchant*, Princes-street.
Baker, Samuel, *Grocer and Tea-dealer*, Wine-street.
Baker, Martha, *Grocer and Tea-dealer*, Ditto.
Baker, Richard, *Carver and Gilder*, 15, Clare-street.
Baker and Co *Linen-merchants*, High-street.
Baker, William, *Taylor*, Bridge-street.
Baker, Joseph, *Cutler and Hardwareman*, Ditto.
Baker, John, *Shoemaker*, 25, Castle-street
Baker, *Lodging-house*, 2, Glocester-place, Clifton.
Baker, Thomas, *Carpenter and Joiner*, Hotwell-road.
Baker, Thomas, *Cabinet-maker*, Ditto.
Baker, Mrs. Ruth, Pipe-lane
Baker, Capt. Valentine, Wells-street
Baker, J Innys, *Merchant*, Lower Maudlin-lane.
Baker, Mrs. Rachael, 52, St. Michael's-hill,
Baker, *Attorney's Stationer*, College-street.
Baker, James, *Ivory and Oval Turner*, Stokes-croft.
Baker, Henry, *Red Lyon*, Tower-lane
Baker, John, *Dealer in Spirits*, Christmas-street.
Baker, William, *Grocer*, West-street.
Baker, Charles, *Seedsman*, Ditto.
Baker, Samuel, *Hat-manufacturer*, 23, Redcliff-street.
Baker, J *Cheesemonger*, 23, Ditto.
Baker, Mary, *Bell*, Cathay.
Baker, Jeremiah, Esq. Redland
Baldwyn, William, *Academy for young Gentlemen*, Lawrence-hill.
Bale, Phillip, *Staffordshire-warehouse*, Bath-street.
Bale, Ann, *Grocer*, Back.

B 2 Bal,

Ball, Capt. Archelaus, Braziers-court, Quay.
Ball, Thomas, *Carpenter*, Hotwell-road.
Ball, Thomas, Gent. Montague-ftreet.
Ball, William, *Maltfter*, Wilder-ftreet.
Ball, William, *Inn-keeper*, Lamb-ftreet.
Ball, Mary, *George*, Temple-ftreet.
Ball, William, *Mafon and Stone-cutter*, Redcliff-back.
Ball, John, *Tennis-court*, Redcliff-hill.
Ballar, John, *Haberdasher*, Wine-ftreet.
Baller, George, *Hair-dreffer*, Caftle-ftreet.
Bally and Kington, *Taylors*, Hope-fquare, Hotwells.
Bally and Hellicar. *Ironmongers*, Thomas-ftreet.
Banfield, Samuel, *White Hart*, Barr's-ftreet.
Banfield, John, *Mariner*, 13, Hanover-ftreet.
Banfield, Thomas, *Hooper*, Weft-ftreet.
Banfield, John, *White Hart*, Avon-ftreet.
Banfield, Evar, *Joiner*, 99 Redcliff-ftreet.
Bangley, Coathupe and Co *Coopers, and Cyder-merchants*, Lewins-
    mead.
Banifter, John, *Diftiller*, Broad-mead.
Banifter, Mrs. Ann, 23, Trinity-ftreet.
Banifter, George, *Carver*, College-ftreet.
Banks, John, *General Draper*, Hotwell-road.
Bantlev and Wigan, *Diftillers*, Great-gardens.
Baram, Mary, *Lodging-houfe*, Clifton-hill.
Barber, William and Son, *Maltfters*, Redcliff-hill.
Barber, Mr. James, jun. 5, Bedminfter-caufeway.
Barlow, James, *Wharfinger*, under the Bank,
Barlow, Thomas, *Black-fmith*, Bedminfter.
Barlow, Robert, *Ship*, Glocefter-lane.
Barnes, John, *Rifing Sun*, Weft-ftreet.
Barnes, Mrs. Ann, 78, Lewins-mead.
Barnes, John, *Latin Teacher and Accomptant*, Kingfdown-parade.
Barnes, William, Efq. Redland.
Barnes, Henry, Gent. King-ftreet.
Barrell, Benjamin, *Smith and Farrier*, Temple-ftreet,
Barrow, John, *Merchant*, 17, College-green.
Barrow, Mrs. Hefter, Culver-ftreet.
Barrow, Jofeph, *Currier*, Redcliff-ftreet.
Barry, Edward, *Bright-fmith*, Marfh-ftreet
Barry, B. *Bookbinder and Stationer*, Briftol-bridge.
Bartlett, John, *Vintner, and Dealer in Spirits*, Hotwell-road.
Bartlett, John, *Surgeon-dentift*, Denmark-ftreet.
Bartlett, Mr. Charles, Small-ftreet
Bartlett, Robert, *Butcher*, Chriftmas-ftreet.

Bartlett,

Bartlett, Mary, *Lamb Inn*, Weft-ftreet.
Bartlett, William, *Brandy-merchant*, Thomas-ftreet.
Bartley, William, *Diftiller*, Redcrofs-ftreet.
Bartley, Mr. Nehemia, Temple-ftreet
Bafcomb, Francis, *Seven Stars*, Penn-Street.
Bafkerville, Francis, *Gardener*, Stapleton-road.
Baftable, John, *Carpenter*, 8, Caftle-ditch
Baftable, Jonathan, *Coach-carver*, Milk-ftreet.
Baftable, Ephraim, *Stay-maker*, Old-market.
Baftable, Efarhadden, *Cabinet-maker*, Newgate-ftreet.
Bate, Roger, *Salutation Tavern*, Hotwell-road.
Bates, Thomas, *Carpenter*, Charles-ftreet.
Bath, Shurmur, *Maltfter*, Stokes-croft.
Bath, Mr Neville, Clifton-hill.
Bath, Neville and Co. *Cutlers, Hardwaremen, and Bright Iron
    mongers*, Thomas-ftreet.
Bateman, Henry, *Old Trout*, Cherry-lane.
Bateman, Richard, *Excife-officer*, Diltons-court.
Batt, Thomas, *Ship*, 14, Princes-ftreet.
Batten, William, *Grocer and Tea-dealer*, Barton.
Battens, William, *Writing-mafter*, Cyder-houfe-paffage.
Batterfby, Mr. William, 3, St James's-fquare.
Bawker, William, *Accomptant*, Pembroke-court,
Bawn, William, *Teacher of Navigation*, King-ftreet.
Baxter, John, *Turner*, Penn-ftreet.
Baxter, Capt. Robert, 6, Pipe-lane.
Baylis, W. and T. *Wholefale Linen-drapers*, Wine-ftreet.
Bayly, George, *Taylor*, Lower Maudlin-lane.
Bavly, Robert and Co. *Lead-merchants*, Upper Eafton.
Baynham, Thomas, *Grocer*, Maryport-Street.
Bazeon, Mrs   18, Paul-ftreet.
Bazley, William and Co. *Linen-drapers*, Bridge-parade
Beach, A. and S. *Boarding-fchool for young Ladies*, Somerfet-
    fquare.
Beach and Powell, *Patent Iron fan-light manufactory*, Denmark-
    ftreet, and St. Stephen's avenue.
Beacham, Phillip, *Tenniscourt*, Bedminfter.
Beale, William, *Night Conftable*, Caftle-green.
Beams, S. Albemarle-lodge, Albemarle-row.
Beard, William, *Baker*, Redliff-hill.
Beaven, Jofeph, *Sadler and Bridle-cutter*, Thomas-ftreet.
Beaufoy, Mrs. S. 6, Stokes-croft.
Becher, Granfield, Efq 12, College-green.
Beck, Mrs.   25, King-fquare
Beck, John, *Hofier*, 95, Redcliff-ftreet.

                                               Becket,

Becket, John Brice, *Stationer*, Corn-ſtreet.
Beddome, Croſs and Co. *Oilmen*, Small-ſtreet.
Beddome, Miſs Jane, 14, Park.
Belamy, John, *Butcher*, Bedminſter.
Bell, Heſter, *Lodging-houſe*, Bell-avenue, Quay.
Bell, John William, *Portrait-painter*, Albemarle-lodge, Hotwells.
Bell, Francis, *Lodging-houſe*, 6, Denmark-ſtreet.
Belſher, Benjamin, *Cabinet-maker and Auctioneer*, Bridge-ſtreet.
Belcher, James, *Apple Tree*, Broad-mead.
Bence, I. B. *Shoe-warehouſe*, Wine-ſtreet
Bence, Mr. I. B. Berkely-ſquare.
Bengough, Henry, Eſq. St. James's-ſquare.
Bengough, George, Eſq. Duke-ſtreet.
Beniſon, George and William, *Braziers*, Baldwin-ſtreet.
Bennet, James and John, *Wool-ſtaplers*, Bedminſter.
Bennett, William, *Yeoman*, Redland.
Bennett, John, *Glazier*, Griffin-lane.
Bennett, Thomas, *Hour-glaſs maker*, Bridewell-lane.
Bennett, Richard, *Taylor*, Old-market
Bennett, John, *Hat-manufacturer*, New-ſtreet.
Bennett, Thomas, *Accomptant*, 20, Guinea-ſtreet.
Berjew, Mrs.   5, Dighton-ſtreet.
Berkin, William, Gent. Clifton-hill.
Bernard, Abraham, *Silverſmith*, High-ſtreet.
Berry,   *Lodging-houſe*, 2, Sion-row.
Berry, Charles, Gent Gloceſter-lane.
Reſt, William, *Linen-draper*, Hotwell-houſe.
Beſſom, Thomas, *Exciſe-officer*, Cathay.
Bethel, Richard, *Full Moon*, Cheeſe-lane.
Bettington, Joſeph, *Tyler, Plaiſterer and Painter*, Limekiln-lane.
Bettington, John, *Merchant*, Upper Eaſton.
Bevan, James, *Dealer in Spirits*, Milk-ſtreet.
Bevan, William, *Umbrella-maker*, Back.
Bevan, Elizabeth, *Ship*, Butts.
Bevan, Mr. George, Small-ſtreet.
Bevan and Stringer, *Stay-makers*, Hillgrove-ſtreet.
Bevan, John, *Shoe-maker*, Giant's Caſtle, Temple-ſtreet.
Pevan, Mrs. Eleanor, Cathay.
Bevan, John, *Cabinet-maker*, Merchant-ſtreet.
Bewley, Ann, *Queens Head*, Upper Eaſton.
Bicket, John, *Paſtry-cook and Confectioner*, Redcliff-ſtreet.
Bickley, Benjamin, *Merchant*. Princes-ſtreet.
Bicknell, John, *Baker*, Redcliff-ſtreet.
Biddeil, Charles, *Carpenter and Builder*, Milk-ſtreet.
Biddoe, Thomas, *Sugar-refiner*, Gloceſter-ſtreet.

                                              Bidmead

Bidmead, John, *House and Timber-measurer*, Balloon-court, Wilder-street.

Biggs, Samuel, *Merchant*, Glocester-street.

Biggs and Popham, *Merchants*, Queen-square.

Biggs, Robert, *Cheese-factor*, Back.

Biggs, Benjamin, *Linen-draper*, High-street.

Biggs,   *Earthen-ware shop*, Maryport-street.

Biggs, Thomas, *Lodging-house*, 3, Princes-place, Clifton

Biggs, George, *Accomptant*, 27, Charles-street.

Biggs, James, *Stay-maker*, 28, Ditto.

Billing, William, *Baker*, Broad-mead.

Bingham, John, *Dealer in Spirits*, Maryport-street.

Birch, Mr. Charles, Dove-street.

Birch, Mrs. Martha, 4, Gay-street.

Birch, Savage and Co. *Grocers*, Small-street.

Birch and Savage, *Grocers*, Ditto.

Bird, Edward, *Watch-maker*, 16, Clare-street.

Bird, Hawkins, *Tea-dealer*, Wine-street.

Bird, Thomas, *Carpenter*, Oxford-street.

Bird, Joseph, *Blackmoores-head*, Lawrence-hill.

Bird, Joseph, *Turner*, Baldwin-street.

Bird, John, *Gardener*, Stapleton-road.

Birt, John, *Gardener*, Redland.

Birt, Paul, *Brandy-merchant*, Maryport-street.

Birtill, John, *Currier*, Redcliff-street.

Birtill, John, *Currier*, Baldwin-street.

Bishop, Daniel, *Baker*, 31, Broad-street.

Bishop, George, *Baker*, Host-street.

Bishop, Mr. Samuel, Counter-slip.

Bishop, Mr. John, Temple-street.

Bishop, Samuel and John, *Skinners and Parchment-makers*, Tower-street, Great-gardens.

Bishop, John, *Broker*, Ditto.

Bishop, William, *Fox and Hounds*, Redcliff-street.

Bishop, John, *Dealer in Spirits*, Broad-mead.

Biss, John, Gent. Cotham-hill.

Biss, John, *Taylor*, Montague-street.

Biss, Mrs. Rebecca, Eugene-street.

Bissix, Rachael and Sons, *Sugar-refiners*, Temple-street.

Blackmore, Hester, *Lodging-house*, Cathay.

Blackwell, Thomas, Esq Park-row.

Blackwood, Miss   Clifton-down.

Blagden, Thomas, Gent. College-green.

Blake, John, *Mariner*, Culver-street.

Blakely, James, *Blackmoores-head*, Bath-street.

Blurch,

Blanch, Thomas, *Heel and Patten-maker*, Merchant-street.
Blanch, John, Gent. College-street.
Blanning, Richard, *Silk-dyer and Callenderer*, Milk-street.
Blanning, Nicholas, *Ship-builder*, Redcliff-hill.
Blanning, William, *Ship-builder*, Wapping.
Blesher, Elizabeth, *Butcher*, St. James's-back.
Bletchley, John, *Linen-draper*, High-street.
Blethin, Mr. John, 40, Castle-green.
Blissett, Mrs.   Clifton-down.
Bladen, William, *Lodging-he.p.* 2, Glocester-place, Clifton.
Bobbett, William, *Baker*, West-street.
Bodman, Mrs. Mary, St. Michaels-hill.
Body, Henry, *Jack-maker*, Milk-street.
Boley, Robert, *Oil and Colourman*, Peter-street.
Bomand, Richard, *Excise-officer*, Rack-close.
Bond, Charles, *Livery Stable-keeper*, Clifton-hill.
Bones, Thomas, *General Bakery*, Quay.
Bonner, Samuel, *Printer of the Bristol Journal*, Castle-green.
Bonville, Thomas, *Merchant*, St. James's-square.
Boon, Johanna, *Staffordshire-warehouse*, Maryport-street.
Boord and Hill, *Woollen-drapers*, Wine-street.
Booth, Thomas, *Broker*, 3, Montague-street; office in Corn-
     street.
Booth, Timothy, *Black-horse Inn*, West-street.
Booth, George, *Broker*, Thomas-street.
Booth, Eleanor, *Butcher*, Temple-street.
Bosher, Charles, *Silk-dyer*, Castle-ditch.
Boston, Mrs. Hannah, Hillgrove-street.
Boabier, William, *Malifter*, 2, Avon-street.
Boucher, Richard, Gent. Clifton.
Bould and Maund, *Tea-dealers*, Maryport-street.
Boulster, Jane, *School for young Ladies*, Limekiln lane.
Bourne, William, *Accomptant*, Redcross-street.
Bowden, Samuel, *Wire-merchant*, St. Augustins-place.
Bowden, Richard, *Cooper*, Baldwin-street.
Bowdich, Thomas and Co. *Hat-manufacturers*, Clare-street.
Bowen, Mathewsalem, *Hole in the Wall*, Princes-street.
Bowen, Mrs. E. *Lodgings* 4 & 5, Princes-place, Clifton.
Bowen, Mrs. Mary, 18, College-green.
Bowen, Mr. John, 2, Hanover-street.
Bowen, Mrs. Mary, 16, Bedminster-causeway.
Bowen, Mr. Perigrine, St. Michaels-hill.
Bowen, Miss. Rebecca, Temple-street.
Bower, Joseph, *Accomptant*, Park-row.
Bower, John, *Accomptant*, Jamaica-street.

                                        Bower,

Bower, James, *Ironmonger*, Redcliff-ftreet.
Bower, James, *Gunpowder-office*, Exchange.
Bowet,   *Lodging-houfe*, Rownham-paffage.
Bowles, Edward, Efq. Royal Fort.
Bowman, James, *New Inn* Dowry-fquare.
Bowman, John and Co. *Hog-butchers*, Weft-ftreet.
Bowman, Robert, *Hog-butcher*, Wade-ftreet.
Bowfer, William, *Accomptant*, Horfe-fair.
Boyer, Mrs. *Boarding-fchool for young Ladies*, Clifton.
Boyle, Daniel, *Hair-dreffer*, 51, Princes-ftreet.
Boyton,   *Organift*, Charlotte-ftreet.
Brace, Richard, *Mariner*, under the Bank.
Bracey, Thomas, *Butcher*, Butcher-row.
Braden, John, *Shoe-maker*, Stokes-croft.
Bradley, John, *Hat-manufacturer*, Montague-ftreet.
Bradley, Elizabeth, *Haberdafher*, 66, Caftle-ftreet.
Brain, Mary, *Mantua-maker*, 11, Caftle-green.
Brain, Thomas, *Wholefale Quarrier*, Lawrence-hill.
Bratt, Thomas, *Hair-dreffer*, Dove-ftreet.
Breffett, Mrs Elizabeth, 4, Butts.
Brent, Thomas, *Butcher*, Thomas-ftreet.
Brett, William, *Duke's-head*, King-ftreet.
Brevell,   *Bifcuit-baker and Confectioner*, Penn-ftreet.
Brewer, Jofeph, *Taylor*, 17, Denmark-ftreet.
Brewer, William, *Tea-dealer*, Union-ftreet.
Brice, Edward and Nathaniel, *Sugar-refiners*, Old-market.
Brice, Mr. Samuel, Old-market
Brice, Worthington, *Merchant*, 36, Princes-ftreet.
Brice, William, *Trunk-maker*, Corn-ftreet.
Brickendon, Mrs. *Lodging-houfe*, St. Vincents-parade, Hotwells.
Bridges, John, *Soap and Candle-manufacturer*, Hotwell-road.
Bright, Lowbridge, Efq. Great George-ftreet.
Bright, Richard, *Merchant*, 27, Queen-fquare.
Bright, Henry and Co. *Sugar-refiners*, Counter-flip.
Brimble, John, *Watch-maker*, Redcliff-hill.
Brimble, Mrs. Alice, Old-market.
Brittan, Benjamin, *Accomptant*, Pembroke-court.
Brittan, John, Gent. Ditto.
Broad, James, *Mafon*, Rofemary-ftreet.
Brock, Benjamin, Gent. Kingfdown-parade.
Brock, Thomas, *Silverfmith*, 1, Wine-ftreet.
Broderip, John, *Three Sugar-loaves*, Marfh-ftreet.
Broderip, Mrs. Hefter, 1, Gay-ftreet.
Bromhead, Thomas, *Taylor*, Stokes-croft.
Bromley, Mifs, *School for young Ladies*, St. Michaels-hill.

C

Brookman,

Brookman, William, *Confectioner*, 101, Redcliff-ftreet.
Brooks, Henry, *Hooper*, Bridewell-lane.
Brooks, H. F. and Co. *Merchants*, St. John's-bridge.
Brooks, Henry, *Merchant*, Ditto.
Brooks, Mr William, Lamb-ftreet.
Brooks, Mary, *Bacchus*, Temple-ftreet.
Brooks, Thomas, *Toy-maker* Ditto.
Brooks, Solomon, *Sheriff's-officer*, Bedminfter.
Brooks, Samuel, *Cuftom-houfe officer*, College-green.
Broom, Jofeph Inall. *Brafs-founder*, 66, Caftle-ftreet.
Broom, Robert, *Full-moon Inn*, North-ftreet.
Broom, Price, and Co *Ironmongers*, Clare-ftreet.
Brotherton, Matthew, *Lodging-houfe*, 1, Hotwell-parade.
Broughton, Mrs Sarah, Redcliff-hill
Brown and Granger, *Ironmongers*, Bridge-ftreet.
Brown, Samuel, *Accomptant*, Hotwell-road.
Brown, John, *Accomptant* 24, College-ftreet.
Brown, Lettice, *Lodging-houfe*, 5, College-green.
Brown, Mrs H. Griffin-lane.
Brown, Mrs E. 3, Beaufort-court.
Brown, Mrs. Unus, Wilder-ftreet.
Brown, Edward, *Sugar-loaf*, Bridewell-lane.
Brown, Jofeph, *Heel-cutter*, Lewins-mead.
Brown, John William *Hair-dreffer*, Narrow Wine-ftreet.
Brown, Richard, *Cabinet-maker*, Old-market.
Brown, William, *Accomptant*, Elbroad-ftreet.
Brown, William, *Pork-butcher*, Nicholas-ftreet.
Brown, Jofeph, *Butcher*, Butcher-row.
Brown, John, *Hair-dreffer*, St. James's-back.
Brown, Ebenezer, *Tanner*, River-ftreet.
Brown, M and H. *Grocers*, 89, Redcliff-ftreet.
Brown, John, *Carver and Gilder*, Church-ftreet, St. Stephen's
Brown, Mr James, Redcliff-parade
Brown, Mrs.   2, Somerfet-fquare.
Brown, Mrs. Mary, Berkely-fquare.
Brown, John, *Taylor and Stay-maker*, 5, Broad-mead.
Brown, John, *Lamb Inn*, Ditto,
Brown, William, *Wine-cooper*, Elbroad-ftreet.
Browne, Sufannah and Son, *Painters*, Quay.
Browne, William, *Bookfeller and Stationer*, Tolzey.
Browne, William, *Adam and Eve*, Wine-ftreet.
Brownfcomb,   *Dealer in Spirits*, Thomas-ftreet.
Bubb, Mrs. Eliza, 80, Lewins-mead.
Buckingham, Mr James, Baptift-mills.
Budd, William, *Taylor*, Frog-lane.

Budget.

Budget, Joseph, *Dealer in Horfes*, Bedminfter.

Bulgin and Sheppard, *Booksellers and Stationers*, Wine-ftreet.

Bulgin and Roffer, *Printers of the Briftol Mercury*, Broad-ftreet.

Bulgin, Mr. William, Duke-ftreet.

Bull, Mrs. Ann, Stokes-croft.

Bull, Mrs. Mary, Redcrofs-ftreet.

Bull, George, *Patten-maker*, 34, Redcliff-ftreet.

Bullen, George, *Glazier and Painter*, Hotwell-road.

Bullen, Henry, *Glazier*, Temple-ftreet.

Bullen, James, *Cabinet maker*, Bridge ftreet.

Bulley, Elizabeth, *Pawnbroker*, Temple-ftreet

Bullock, Elizabeth, *China and Tea-warehoufe*, H gh-ftreet.

Bullock, Mifs, *Boarding-fchool for young Ladies*, Barton.

Bullock, Mrs. Sarah, 6, St James's cnurch-vard.

Bullock, George, *Cabinet-moker*, 28, Redcliff-ftreet.

Bullock, Giles, *Baker*, Glocefter-lane

Bullock, Charles, *Accomptant*, Bedminfter-caufeway.

Bulman, Thomas, Gent. 28, Trinity-ftreet.

Bulmer, Edward, Gent. 2, Guinea-ftreet

Bumaford, Thomas, *Cabinet-maker*, Denmark-ftreet.

Bunce, Matthew, *Duke of York Inn*, Thomas-ftreet.

Bundy, Mary, *Lodging-houfe*, 20, Queen-fquare.

Bundy, Benjamin, *Sail-maker*, Princes-ftreet.

Bundy, Mr. Richard, Guinea-ftreet

Burbridge, Elias, *Cuftom-houfe officer*, St James's-parade.

Burden, Philip, *Grocer*, 39, Caftle-ftreet.

Burford, Mrs Sarah, 17, Trinity-ftreet.

Burford, Mr William, Kingfdown parade.

Burford, Francis, Gent. 11, Dighton-ftreet

Burford, Francis, *Golden Heart*, Paffage-ftreet, St. Philip's.

Burge, Thomas, *Hair-dreffer*, Old King-ftreet.

Burge, Richard, *Confectioner*, Back.

Burge, Ifaac, *Paftry-cook and Confectioner*, Corn-ftreet.

Burge, Ann, *Dealer in Spirits* 78, Caftle-ftreet

Burge, Robert, *Taylor*, Green-ftreet, Hotwells.

Burge, Ifaac, *Confectioner and Gingerbread-baker*, St. Auguftines-back.

Burge, Ifaac, *Paftry-cook*, Barton-alley.

Burge, William, *Confectioner*, Weft-ftreet

Burge, William and Co *Soap and Candle-manufacturers*, Ditto

Burge, Ebenezer, *Accomptant*, Un ty-ftreet, St Philip's.

Burge, Robert, *Writing-mafter and Accomptant*, Bedminfter-caufeway.

Burges, Mifs, *Lodging-houfe*, 10, Dovry-fquare.

Burges, Mrs. Catharine, Redcliff-parade.

Burges,

Borges, William, *Accomptant*, 7, Carolina-row.
Burgum, Mrs. Betty, 4, St. James's-parade.
Burgum and Wilkins, *Soap and Candle-manufacturers*, Broad-plain.
Burjoh, John, *Excise-officer*, Eibroad-street.
Burke, Mary, *Orange and Lemon-warehouse*, Quay.
Burleigh, John, *Currier and Leather-cutter*, Castle-green.
Burleigh, Samuel, *Currier and Leather-cutter*, Maryport-street.
Burleigh, James, *Butcher*, Nicholas-street.
Burnell, Robert, *Mealman*, Dolphin-street.
Burnet, Miss, Rod. es-house, Clifton-hill.
Barr, James, *Gent.* Dove-street.
Burrowdale, Capt. Joseph, Stoney-hill.
Burt, Thomas, *Grocer*, Thomas-street.
Burton, Charles, *Hair-dresser and Perfumer*, North-street.
Buse, Mrs. Hester 12, Pipe-lane.
Bush, George, *Lace and Fringe-manufacturer*, Clare-street.
Bush, Robert and Co. *Pewterers, Brass and Copper-smiths*, 20, High-street.
Bush, Mr. William, St. Michaels-hill.
Bush, John, *Lodging-house*, 7, Beaufort-court.
Bush, William, *Merchant*, King-square.
Bush, Hannah, *Corn-factor*, West-street.
Bush, William, *Corn factor*, Nicholas-street.
Bush, Elton and Bush, *Merchants*, Baldwin-street.
Bush, Robert and Co *Copper-smiths*, Thomas-street.
Bush, George, *Esq* Redclift, near Wapping.
Butler, William, *Merchant*, Queen-square.
Butler, Aaron, *Hat-manufacturer*, John-street.
Butler, William, *Brush-maker*, West-street.
Butler, John and William, *Brush-makers*, Broad-mead.
Butts, Mary, *Butcher*, Butcher-row.
Buxam and Broom, *Soap and Candle-manufacturers*, Thomas-street.

C

Cadell, James, *Gent.* 4, Montague-street.
Cadell, Mrs. Martha, Stokes-croft.
Calder, Elisha, *Lodging-house*, 2, Albemarle-row.
Callan. Hester, *Broker*, Thomas-street.
Callen, Richard, *Sugar-loaf*, Back-street.
Campbell, John, *Bacon and Cheese-factor*, Baldwin-street.
Campbell, Richard, *Cabinet-maker and Joiner*, Horse-fair.

Cambridge,

Cambridge, Hefter, *Tea-dealer*, 20, Charles-ftreet.
Camplin, John, *Merchant*, Trinity-ftreet.
Camplin, James, *Watch-maker*, Elbroad-ftreet.
Cannington and Co. *Glafs-manufactu.ers* Temple-ftreet.
Cannon, Michael, *Accomptant*, 11, Hanover-ftreet.
Capel, William, *Shoe-maker*, 51, Redcliff-ftreet.
Carden William, *Linen-draper*, 5, Clare-ftreet.
Cardwell, Thomas, *Hallier*, St. John's-bridge.
Carew, Andrew, *Salesman*, Quay.
Carey, John, *Tobacco-pipe manufacturer*, Old-market.
Carit, James, *Mufician*, Rofe-alley.
Carpenter, Mrs.   38, College-ftreet.
Carrenter, Edward, *Carpenter*, Stokes-croft.
Carpenter, Parfons, and Co. *London Carriers*, Old-market.
Carpenter, Richard, *Carpenter*. Elbroad-ftreet.
Carr, Jofeph, *Deputy Water-bailiff*, King-ftreet.
Carter, Mr. Henry, 19, Somerfet-fquare.
Carter, Edward, *Conveyancer*, 1, Cathay.
Carter, John, *Stay-maker*, Caftle-ditch.
Carter, Nath. Saunders, *Maltfter*, Griffin-lane.
Carter, Blaze, *Cuftom-houfe officer*, Stoney-hill.
Carter, Ann, *Broker*, 18, Peter-ftreet.
Carter, Thomas, *Cheefe-factor*, 29, Broad-ftreet.
Cartwright, Smith and Beddoe, *Sugar-refiners*, Old King-ftreet.
Cafmajor. Mrs. Ann, 60, Queen-fquare.
Caffin, Mr. James, Dove-ftreet.
Caffin, Capt. S. N. Cannon-ftreet.
Caffon, John, *Glafs-polifher*, Jacob-ftreet.
Caftle, Mr. Michael, Cheefe-lane.
Caftle, Jofeph, *Baker*, Broad mead.
Caftle, Robert and Co. *Rectifiers*, Milk-ftreet.
Catcott, George Symes, *Sub-Librarian*, Temple-back.
Cave, Stephen, Efq. Brunfwick-fquare.
Cave, John and Co. *Colour-manufacturers*, Wilder-ftreet.
Cave, Stephen and Co. *Flint and Crown Glafs-mannfactory*,
      Redcliff-back.
Chaddock, James, *Carpenter*, Weft-ftreet.
Chaddock, John, *Accomptant*, 17, Guinea-ftreet.
Challenger, Jeremiah, *Permit-writer*, Caftle-ditch.
Chamberlaine, Edward, *Deputy Searcher*, 2, Queen-fquare.
Chamberlaine, John, *Seedsman*, Weft-ftreet.
Chambers, Mrs Sarah Eafton, 14, Barton.
Chambers, Mark, *Grocer*, Horfe-fair.
Chambers, Henry, *Gardener*, Upper Eafton.
Chambers, James, *Butcher*, Temple-ftreet.

                                    Chambers,

Chambers, John, *Biscuit-baker*, Church-street, St. Stephen's.
Champion, Robert, *Currier*, 43, Castle-street.
Champion, Mr. George, Clifton.
Champion, John, *Merchant*, College-green.
Champion, George, *Tobacco-pipe manufactory*, Redcliff-street.
Champion, William, *Accomptant*, Redcliff-yard.
Chandler, John, *Pump and Block-maker*, Quay.
Chandler, Walter, *Cutler*, 47, Corn-street.
Chandler, John, *Red Lyon*, Castle-street.
Chandler, John, *Ship Joiner*, Currant-lane.
Chandler, Mrs. Unis, Queen-street.
Chapman, Miss,   7, Dowry-square.
Chapman, Ann, *Collenderer*, Stokes-croft.
Chapman, George, *Butcher*, Merchant-street.
Chappel, James, *Ring of Bells*, Thomas-street.
Chappel, Hannah, *Gardener, &c.* Red-hill.
Charles, John, *Grocer*, Clifton-hill.
Charles, and Co. *Patent Block-makers*, Quay.
Charleton, Robert, *Grocer*, 76, Castle-street.
Cherry, John, *Auctioneer*, Broad-street.
Cherry, David, *Presser and Packer*, Small-street, and 8, Tontine-
     warehouse, Quay.
Cheese, William, *Gardener*, North-street, Bedminster.
Cheese, John, *Gardener*, Ditto.
Cheson, William, *George Inn*, Without Temple-gate.
Chiddey,   *Excise-officer*, 3, Kington's-buildings.
Chidgey, Robert, *Shoe-maker*, 9, Peter-street.
Chidgey, John and Henry, *Masons*, Barton-street.
Chilcott, William, *Hallier*, Freshford-alley.
Child, Charles, *Carpenter*, Clarence-place.
Child, William, *Pawn-broker*, 5, St. James's church-yard.
Chubb, John, *Sail-maker*, 25, Princes-street.
Chubb, James, *Excise-officer*, Cannon-street.
Church, William, *Hallier*, Durdham-down.
Churley, George, *Duke of Devonshire*, Great Ann-street.
Churnside, Capt. Thomas, St. Augustines-place.
Claggett, Mrs. S. Upper Maudlin-lane.
Clapp, Mrs. Ann, Clifton.
Claridge, William, *Haberdasher*, Union-street.
Clark, Joan, *Coach-maker*, Milk-street.
Clark, John, *Watch-maker*, Rosemary-street.
Clark, Joseph, *Linen-draper*, 12, Castle-street.
Clark, Mary, *Ship and Dove*, St. Michaels-steps.
Clark, W. N. *Carpenter, and Dealer in Spirits*, Charles-street.
Clark, Sarah, *Lodging-house*, Paul-street.

                                        Clark,

Clark, Mrs. Mary, 5, Portland-ftreet.
Clarke, Thomas, *Cuftom-houfe officer*, Hillgrove-ftreet.
Clarke, Charles, *Writing-mafter*, Caftle-green.
Clark, John, *Druid*, Old-market
Clark, Jofeph, *Corn-factor*, Weft-ftreet.
Clark, John, *Butcher*, Butcher-row.
Clark, Elizabeth, *Wire-worker*, Baldwin-ftreet.
Clark, William, *Glass-cutter and Engraver*, Temple-ftreet.
Clark, James, *Glass-houfe*, Ditto.
Clark, James, *Dealer in Spirits*, Redcliff-ftreet
Clark, Thomas, *Wine-merchant*, Cathay-parade.
Clark, Mrs. Barcella, Bedminfter-caufeway,
Clark, Thomas, *Wheelwright*, Bedminfter.
Clark, Jacob, *Hen and Chickens*, North-ftreet, Bedminfter.
Clark, Thomas, *Taylor*, Quay.
Clarkfon, George, *Accomptant*, Greville-ftreet.
Clatworthy, William, *Taylor*, Limekiln-lane.
Claxton, Robert, Efq. 9, Park-ftreet.
Clayfield, Mary and Son, *Wine and Brandy merchants*, **Caftle-**
ftreet.
Clealand, William, *Cuftom-houfe officer*, Temple-street.
Clement, John, *Pawn-broker*, Ditto
Clement, John, *Plumber*, 125, Redcliff-ftreet.
Clement, Thomas, *Supervifor*, Cathay.
Clevely, Mary, *Peruke-maker*, Chriftmas-street.
Clifford, Thomas, *Nail-maker*, Limekiln-lane.
Clifford, Thomas, *Dealer in Spirits*, Glocefter-lane.
Clift, John, *Linen-draper*, 3, High-street.
Clift, William, *Dealer in Spirits*, Old-market.
Cliffold, Peter and Co. *Rectifiers*, Redcliff-street.
Clootwyk, Merwede Van, Gent. 7, Sion-row.
Clowd, Ann, *Dealer in Spirits*, Silver-street.
Clowes, George, Efq. Kingfdown-parade
Cluett, Thomas, *Shoe-maker*, St. Michaels-hill
Clymer, Marmaduke, *Watch-maker*, 37, High-street.
Coates, Thomas, *Wine-merchant*, Church-street, St. Stephen's.
Codd, Martha, *Lodging-houfe*, 8, Wells-ftreet.
Cole, John, *Accomptant*, Milk-ftreet
Cole, George, *Taylor and Salesman*, Bridge-ftreet
Cole, John, *Builder*, York-place, Clifton.
Cole, Ann, *Lodging-houfe*, Hotwell-road.
Cole, John, *Bread and Biscuit-baker*, Lewins-mead.
Cole, John, *Peftle and Mortar*, Prince Eugean-lane.
Cole, Mr. Thomas, Bedminfter.
Coleman, Robert, Efq. 2, Somerfet-ftreet

Coleman,

Coleman, Robert and Co. *Leicester-warehouse*, Bridge-street.
Coleman, Obedia, *Clock and Watch-maker*, Redcliff-hill.
Collard, Edward, *Butcher*, Temple-street.
Collier, Theodofius *Ironmonger*, Hotwell-road.
Collier,   *Millinery and Tea-shop*, Union-street.
Collins, Francis, *Tobacconist*, 7, Peter-street.
Collins, John, *Accomptant*, Kingsdown-parade.
Collins, Mr. Thomas, 7, Hillgrove-street.
Collins, Robert, *Merchant*, 17, King-square.
Collins, Sarah, *Broker*, Thomas-street.
Collins, William *Wine and Brandy-merchant*, Bath-street.
Collins, Henry, *Skinner*, Wade-street.
Collins, Henry, *Patent Breeches-maker*, Redcliff-street.
Collins, John, *George Inn*, Bedminster.
Comer, John and Son, *Stationers*. Redcliff-street.
Colshier, John, *Lodging-house* Charles-street.
Colston, Richard, *Larding-waiter*, 11, Barton.
Comer, William, *Cheese-factor*, Redcliff-street.
Comer, James, *Stay-maker*, Queen-street.
Comfort, Robert, *Lodging-house*, Hotwell-road.
Coombes, William, *Tin-plate worker*, 16, Castle-street.
Coombes, Edward, *China-mender*, Queen-street.
Coombes, Bartholomew, *King Charles in the Oak*, Bedminster.
Concklin, Berkely, Gent. 25, Queen-square.
Conneby, Richard. *Taylor*, 19, Christmas-street.
Constant, Ann, *Furrier*, Thomas-street.
Conybeare, Samuel, *Taylor*, Quay-street.
Cook, Philip, *Ironmonger*, Back.
Cook, William, *Baker*, King-street.
Cook, Edward, *Three Tuns*, Princes-street.
Cook, Henry and Co. *Sail-makers*, Ditto.
Cook, Henry, *Merchant*, 44, Ditto.
Cooke, John, *Hosier and Glover*, 62, Broad-street.
Cook, Richard, *Baker*, Christmas-street.
Cook, Richard, *Jolly Coombers*, Back-lane.
Cook, Nicholas, *Clothier*, New-street.
Cook, William, *Butcher*, Ditto.
Cook, Thomas, *Bright-smith*, Jacob-street.
Cook, Thomas, *Accomptant*, Avon-street, St. Philip's.
Cock, Diana, *Baker*, Redcliff-street.
Cook, Thomas, *Baker and Corn-factor*, Ditto.
Cooke, Daniel, *Writing-master and Land Surveyor*, 7, Cathay.
Cooke, Isaac, *Attorney*, Berkely-square, office in Corn-street.
Cooke, Mr Richard, Trenchard-lane.
Cooke,   *Corn-factor*, Lodge-street.

                                        Cooke,

Cook, Jacob, *Engraver*, Maryport-church-yard.
Cookworthy, Benjamin, *Haberdasher*, Wine-street.
Cookworthy, Frederick, *Haberdasher and Milliner*, Union-street.
Cooper, Capts. Samuel and George, 23, College-green.
Cooper, Thomas, *Baker*, West-street.
Cooper, Robert, *Dealer in Spirits*, Bowl, Pithay.
Cooper, John, *Shoemaker*, Bath-street.
Cooper, Mary, *Cheese-factor*, Redcliff-street.
Cooper, Capt. William, Prince Amelia's-court, Pipe-lane.
Cooper, Martha, *Greyhound Inn*, Broad-mead.
Cope, Mary, *Tobacco-pipe-maker*, West-street.
Cope, Nathaniel, *Writing-master*, Pile-street.
Copin, Nicholas, *French Stay-maker*, St. Augustine's-back.
Coram, William, *Bear Inn*, Redcliff-street.
Core, Robert, *Hat-manufacturer*, 8, Clare-street.
Corfield, Edward, *Butcher*, Limekiln-lane.
Cork, Joseph, *Coach-master*, Stokes-croft.
Corp, Benjamin, *Carpenter*, Thomas-street.
Corrick, James, *Accomptant*, 29, Princes-street.
Corrick and Chapman, *Cheese-factors*, Nicholas-street.
Corsham, Thomas, *Brandy-merchant*, Thomas-street.
Cory, Nicholas, *Carpenter*, Wilder-street.
Coryndon, George, *Baker*, Bread-street.
Cossens, Joseph, *Bright-smith*, Horse-fair.
Cossens, Nathaniel, *Clock Engraver*, Temple-street.
Cossman, Thomas, *Taylor and Habit-maker*, St. Michaels-hill.
Cottle, Joseph, *Bookseller and Stationer*, 49, High-street.
Cottle, Robert, *Taylor*, 21, Barton.
Cotton, Mary, *Upholder*, 32, Corn-street.
Couch and Farman, *Blue Pennant Quarriers*, St. Philips.
Coulstring, Thomas, *Wire-drawer*, Back.
Coulstring, Mr. James, 19, Orchard-street.
Coulstring, Mr. Thomas, Alfred-place.
Coulstring, Thomas and James, *Cornfactors, Flourmen,* and *Malt-sters,* under the Bank.
Councell, Isabella, *Landscape and Flower-drawer*, Hillgrove-street.
Coupland, George, *White-horse Inn*, Horse-fair.
Course, Charles, *Livery Stable-keeper*, Mews, Sion-row.
Court, John, Gent. Cotham-hill.
Court, William and Charles, *Cabinet-makers, Upholders,* and *Mahogany-merchants,* under the Bank.
Cowen, William, *Mariner*, Bedminster-causeway.
Cowper, Lancelot, *Merchant*, Queen-square.
Cox, Richard, *George Inn*, Castle-street.
Cox Samuel, Esq. Southwell-street.

D   Cox.

Cox, John, *Hair-dreſſer*, St. John's-bridge.
Cox, Chamberlain, *Baker*, Marſh-ſtreet.
Cox, William, *Butcher*, New-ſtreet.
Cox, Charles, *Baker*, Lamb-ſtreet
Cox, James, *Taylor*, Redcliff-hill.
Cox, John, *Hay-dealer*, Bedminſter.
Cozens, Charles and Co. *Tea-dealers*, 7, Broad-ſtreet
Cragg, William, *Ledging-houſe*, Clifton-hill.
Crane, John, *Staymaker*, 2, New-ſtreet.
Crane, Peter, *Cabinet-maker*, Cathay.
Crargle, Capt. Michael, Bull-avenue
Crawley, William, *Hat-manufacturer*, Quakers-bridge.
Cray, Maxull, Gent. St. Philips-place
Creed, Edward, *Globe Inn*, Bedminſter
Crew, Samuel, Gent. 10, Somerſet-ſquare.
Cridland, Samuel, *Golden Anchor*, Guinea-ſtreet.
Crinks, Samuel, *Pot-maker and Major for Glaſs-works*, St Philips
Criſp, Thomas, *Pack-horſe*, Lawrence-hill.
Crocker, John, Gent. 2, College-ſtreet.
Crocker, Capt. Thomas, 6, Ditto.
Crocker, Mr. Philip, Stokes-croft.
Crocker, James, *Smith*, Weſt-ſtreet.
Crocker, John, *Carpenter and Joiner*, Temple-ſtreet.
Croden, James, *Malſter*, Broad-plain.
Cropper, Edward, *Merchant*, 27, Queen-ſquare.
Cropper, Edward and Co. *Soap and Candle-manufacturers*, Chriſt-
mas-ſtreet
Croſs, Mr. John, Small-ſtreet
Croſs, James, *Painter*, Lower Maudlin-lane.
Croſs, Harris, and Co. *Diſtillers*, Temple-backs.
Croſs, William, *Shipwright*, Wapping
Crouch, John, *Trunk-maker*, St. Auguſtines-back.
Crouzet, John, *Card and Paſteboard-manufacturer*, Redcliff-ſtreet.
Crump, Richard, *Tin-plate worker*, Ditto
Cruzet, John, *Gingerbread-baker*, Queen-ſtreet
Cuddeford, Amelia, *Swan Inn*, Maryport-ſtreet.
Culliford, Ann, *Stay-maker*, 6, Ditto.
Culliford, Thomas, *Merchant*, Clifton.
Cullis, John, *Ship-broker*, Quay
Culverwell, Thomas, *Reap-maker*, Nicholas-ſtreet
Culverworth, James, *Crown*, Jamaica-ſtreet.
Curry, Stephen, *Wire-worker*, Baldwin-ſtreet.
Cummins, John, *Looking-glaſs-maker*, Redcroſs-ſtreet.
Cunningham, Capt. Patrick, Eugean-ſtreet
Cunningham, Mary, *Tin plate worker*, Redcliff-ſtreet.

Curtis

Curtis, Johanna, *Assembly coffee-house*, Quay.
Curtis, Robert and Co *Cheese and Butter-factors*, Peter-ftreet.
Curtis, Thomas, *Hair-dreffer*, Narrow Wine-ftreet
Curtis, Jofeph, *Carpenter*, Pithay.
Curtis, Johanna, *Cheefe-factor*, Nicholas-ftreet.
Curtis, John, *Staffordfhire-warehoufe*, Redcliff-ftreet.
Cufick, Amey, *Lodging-houfe*, Hanover-ftreet.
Cutt, Robert, *Fifhmonger*, Baldwin-ftreet.

D

Dagge, Ann, *Midwife*, 7, Broad-plain.
Dallaway, Mofes, *Tyler, Plaifterer and Painter*, Redcliff-ftreet.
Daltera and Roche, *Merchants*, Church-ftreet, St. Stephens.
Dalton, Mr   *Hotel*, Clifton Down,
Dalton, Martha, *Milliner and Haberdafher*, Ditto.
Dardo, Jofiah, *Accomptant*, Peter-ftreet.
Dando, George, *Wheelwright*, Short-grove, Durdham-down.
Daniel, Harford, Weare and Payne, *Iron-merchants*, Quay
Daniel, Phenedus, *Watch-maker and Engraver*, Clare-ftreet.
Daniel, Thomas, *Merchant*, 3, Unity-ftreet.
Daniel, Robert, *Livery Stable-keeper*, 17, King ftreet.
Daniel, William, Efq. Upper Maudlin-lane
Daniel, Daniel, *Horn-worker*, Elbroad-ftreet.
Daniel, Jofeph, *Painter*, 28, Redcrofs-ftreet.
Daniel, Mofes and Co *Mahogany-merchants*, Marybufh-lane.
Daniel, Philip, *China-mender*, Jacob-ftreet.
Daniel, William, *Squirrel*, Bedminfter-caufeway.
D'Anouille,   *Milliner*, 24, St. Auguftines-back.
Danfon, John, *Mariner*, Park.
Darby, Henry, *Baker*, St. Michaels-hill.
Darvill, Sarah, *Rofe and Crown*, St. James's church-yard.
Daubeny, John, Efq. Berkelv-fquare.
Daubeny, Andrew, Efq. 5, King-fquare,
Daubeny and Harris, *Sugar-refiners*, Bridewell-lane.
Daubeny, George, Efq Redland.
David and Hofier, *Silk-mercers*, 46, High-street.
David, Ann, *Mantua-maker*, Old-market
Davis, Lewis, *Shopkeeper*, Newfoundland-ftreet.
Davis, Thomas, *Taylor*, Old King-ftreet.
Davis, Daniel, *Taylor*, Rofemary-ftreet.
Davis, Gifford, *Carpenter and Builder*, Queen fquare.
Davis, John, Efq *Collector of Excife duties*, Ditto
Davis, john and Benjamin, *Tobacconifts*, Back

Davis,

Davis, Martha, *Timber-dealer*, Back.
Davis, Margaret, *Cross Keys*, Ditto.
Davis, Mary, *Lodging-house*, King-ftreet.
Davis, Edward, *Cooper*, 34, Princes-ftreet.
Davis, Elizabeth, *Tea-dealer*, Quay.
Davis, Thomas, *Crow*, Guard-houfe.
Davis, John, *Tin-plate worker*, 11, Peter-ftreet.
Davis, Catharine, *Butcher*, Ditto.
Davis, Mrs. *Lodging-house*, Hotwells.
Davis, S. *Lodging-house*, 5, Hope-fquare.
Davis, Thomas, *Cooper*, Two Nag's-heads, Hotwell-road.
Davis, John, Gent. 13, Park-ftreet.
Davis, Mary, *Upholder and Cabinet-maker*, St. Auguftines-back.
Davis, John, *Porter-house*, under the Bank.
Davis, Henry and Sons, *Bankers*, Small-ftreet.
Davis, Mifs, *Boarding-fchool for young Ladies*, Park-row.
Davis, William, *Cuftom-house officer*, Park.
Davis, Jofeph, *Builder*, 7, Kington's-buildings.
Davis, James, *Leather-merchant*, Kingfdown-parade.
Davis, Michael, *Carpenter*, Ditto.
Davis, Edward, *Stay-maker*, 1, Barton-ftreet.
Davis, John, *Turner*, Old-market.
Davis, Hopkin, *Carpenter*, Daitons-court.
Davis, Mr. Jofeph, 32, Stokes-croft.
Davis, Michael, *Taylor*, Cannon-ftreet.
Davis, William, *Butcher*, Broad Ware.
Davis, John, *Accomptant*, Ditto.
Davis, Jofeph, *Tyler and Plaifterer*, Old-market.
Davis, John, *Butcher*, 1, Weft-ftreet.
Davis, Henry, *Nurfery and Seedsman*, Lawrence-hill.
Davis, Thomas, *Butcher*, Butcher-row.
Davis, Catharine, *Hair-cloth manufacturer*, Glocefter-lane.
Davis, Thomas, *Banker*, Whitehall.
Davis, Robert, *Carpenter and Joiner*, Broad-plain.
Davis, John, *Accomptant*, St. Philips-place.
Davis, John Collaby, *Excise-officer*, St. Philips.
Davis, William, *Mason*, Bath-ftreet.
Davis, John, *Crown and Stars*, Temple-ftreet.
Davis, William, *Baker*,   Ditto.
Davis, David, *Brufh and Sieve-maker*, 127, Redcliff-ftreet.
Davis, Thomas, *Mariner*, 18, Cathay.
Davis, Jacob, *Soap-boiler and Tallow-chandler*, Bedminfter.
Dawes, John, *Farrier*, St. Michaels-hill.
Dawkins, William, *Taylor*, 2, Bloomfbury-buildiugs.
Day, John, *Carpenter and Builder*, Milk-ftreet.

Day,

Day, William, *Child-bed Linen-warehouse*, Bridge-ſtreet.
Day, Thomas, *Corn-meter*, 30, College-ſtreet.
Day, Anthony, *Cabinet-maker*, Gloceſter-lane.
Day, William, *New Inn*, Bedminſter.
Deacon, Zephania, *Cabinet-maker and Joiner*, St. Michaels-hill.
Deak, Capt. Thomas, Bedminſter.
Dealy, Cornelius, *Horn-worker*, Bridewell-lane.
Deane, Whitehead, and Co. *Bankers*, Corn-ſtreet.
Deane, Peter, *Potter*, Boot-lane, Bedminſter.
Deane, Thomas, *Merchant*, 35, Princes-ſtreet.
Debatour, Capt. William, Hanover-ſtreet.
Deeble, T. A. *Engraver*, John-ſtreet.
Deere, Robert, *Glazier and Painter*, 23, Broad-ſtreet.
Delatouche, Henry, *Dancing-maſter*, Bedminſter.
Denner, Thomas, *Corn and Butter-factor*, King-ſtreet.
Dennis, Richard, *Maſon*, Trenchard-lane.
Denniſon, James, *Gardener*, Bedminſter.
Derrick, Elizabeth, *Gingerbread-baker*, Temple-ſtreet.
De Soyres, Rev. Francis, *French Boarding-ſchool*, Park.
Deverell, John, Eſq. Clifton-hill.
Devereux, Sarah, *Ship*, 37, Redcliff-ſtreet.
Devereux, Capt. Stephen, Merchant-ſtreet.
Devoniſh, Capt. John Parrot, Lower-green.
Dibbin, William, *Accomptant*, Thomas-ſtreet.
Dickenſon, Benjamin, *Tobacco-officer*, Elbroad-ſtreet.
Dighton, Mr. William, 4, Dighton-ſtreet.
Dillon, Richard, *Gardener*, Bedminſter.
Dimond, James, *Perfumer*, 20, Clare-ſtreet.
Doddrell, Edward, *Taylor*, Lewins-mead.
Doddrell, John, *Engraver*, Avon-ſtreet.
Doddridge, Jane, *Milliner*, St. Michaels-hill.
Donne, Benjamin, *Teacher of the Mathematics*, Park.
Donne, Benjamin, jun. *Teacher of the Mathematics*, Montague-ſtr.
Doughty, Edward, *Wharfinger*, Quay.
Douglas, Capt. John, Horfield-road.
Dowell, James, *Ironmonger*, 87, Caſtle-ſtreet.
Dowell, Gardener, and Co. *Hat-manufacturers*, Wine-ſtreet.
Dowell, John, *Hair-dreſſer*, St. Johns-bridge.
Doyle, Bartholomew, *Accomptant*, Redcliff-ſtreet.
Drew, Capt. James, 7, Montague-ſtreet.
Driſcoll, Capt. Patrick, 24, College-ſtreet.
Driver, William, *Keeper of Newgate*, Narrow Wine-ſtreet.
Driver, Richard, *Cabinet-maker*, Thomas-ſtreet.
Drury, Harry, *Plow*, Ditto.
Duckett, Capt. Henry, 27, College-ſtreet.

Dudley,

Dudley, Edward, *Farrier*, Glocefter-lane.
Dudley, Thomas, *Lock-smith*, Brick-ftreet.
Dudley, John, *Black-fmith*, Pile-ftreet.
Duff, Thomas, *Scrivener*, Back.
Duffet, James, *Sail-maker*, Stoney-hill.
Duffet, Jofiah, *Potter*, St. Philips.
Duffet, William, *Hat-maker*, Broad-mead.
Dugdale, Elizabeth, *Grocer*, 11, Weft-ftreet.
Duggan, Walter, *Accomptant*, Narrow Wine-ftreet.
Duncomb, David, Gent. Culver-ftreet.
Dunn, John, *Sworn-measurer*, Glocefter-lane.
Dunn, Richard, *Sugar-loaf*, Lower Eafton.
Dupont, John, Gent. Hotwell-parade.
Durban, Richard, *Academy for young Gentlemen*, College-ftreet
Durbin, Sir John, Knt. College-green.
Durbin, Henry, Efq. Bedminfter.
Duval, John, *Hair-dreffer*, St. Michaels-hill.
Dwyer, James, *Hat-maker*, 43, Quay.
Dwyer, James, *Fountain*, Quay.
Dyer, Jofeph, *Diftiller*, 98, Redcliff-ftreet.
Dyer, Sarah, *Tea-deol r.* 3, Broad-ftreet
Dyer, Jane, *China and Glass-warehouse*, Ditto.
Dyer, Samuel, *Currier and Leather-cutter*, 87, Caftle-ftreet
Dyer, Mrs. Ann, 24, Trinity-ftreet.
Dyer, Ann, *Lodging-houfe*, Queen-fquare.
Dyer, William, Gent Small-ftreet.
Dyer, Ann, *Grocer and Cheefe-factor*, Weft-ftreet
Dyer, Mr William, 5, Redcliff-parade.
Dyer, Jonathan, *Houfe and Sign-painter*, Merchant-ftreet.
Dyer. Robert, *Insurance-broker*, Exchange, and 19, Somerfet-ftr
Dyke, John, *Grocer*, Weft-ftreet.
Dymock, Samuel, *Oilman and Lamp-contractor*, Milk-ftreet

E

Eager, George, *Pawnbroker*, Back-ftreet.
Eagles, William, *Carolina Merchant*, Counter-flip.
Eagles, Thomas, *Merchant*, Park-ftreet.
Eagles, Thomas and Co. *Deal-merchants*, Cannons-marfh.
Eames, John, *Wine-merchant*, 9, Queen-fquare.
Eames, Nicholas, *Mariner*, Griffin-lane.
Eames, William, *Baker*, Back-ftreet.
Earl, William, *Tin-plate worker*, Maryport-ftreet.
Eafterbrook, Samuel, *Lebeck-houfe*, Stapleton-road.
Eafterbrook

Asterbrook, Rees, and Co. *Snuff-makers and Tobacconists*, Old-market

aton, Ralph, *Baker*, 26, Hillgrove-street.

aton, George, *Iron-merchant*, Thomas-street.

aton, John, Gent. Lodge-street

Iden, Rev. Thomas, Whitehall Academy.

Edgar, Robert Cann, Efq Griffin-lane.

Edgar, Mr. Prefton, 13, Park.

Edg, Curtis, and Co *Pewterers, Worm-makers, and Copper-smiths*, Temple-street

Edgecumbe, John, *Clock and Watch-maker*, Old-market.

Edgell, James, *Corn-chandler*, 45, Ditto.

Edgell, Jofeph, *Conveyancer*, Greville-street.

Edgell, Chaftin, Efq. Clifton.

Edgell, Thomas, *Wine-drawer*, Milk-street.

Edkins, Michael, *Painter*, 37, Bridge-street

Elkins, Ann, *Boarding-fchool*, Oxford-street.

Edmunds, William, *Mason*, Duck-lane.

Edmunds, Jeremiah, *Accomptant*, 11, Newfoundland-street.

Edmunds, Thomas, *Accomptant*, Jacob-street

Edfon, Dennis, *Surveyor and Engineer*, York-street.

Edwards, William, *Linen-draper*, 10, High-street.

Edwards, Jacob, *Grocer*, 49, Princes-street.

Edwards, James, *Land Surveyor*, Dowry-fquare

Edwards, William and Son, *Shoe makers*, Clare-street.

Edwards, John, *Shoemaker*, St. Michaels-hill

Edwards, Ann, *Sea-horse*, Upper Maudlin-lane.

Edwards, James, *Carpenter*, 10, Oxford-street.

Edwards, William, *Maltfter and Brewer*, Stokes-croft.

Edwards, Thomas, *New Inn*, Hoft-street.

Edwards, Stephen, *Hair-dreffer*, Thomas-street.

Edwards, Jofeph, *Tobacco-pipe maker*, Temple-street.

Edwards, Samuel, Efq Cotham-houfe

Edwards, Tozer, and Co. *Hat-manufacturers*, 81, Caftle-street.

Edye, Jofeph, *Barker*, 18, Corn-street.

Edye, George, *Carpenter and Joiner*, Limekiln-lane.

Elliott, Philip, *China and Tea-warehoufe*, Clare-street

Elliott, Robert, *Hair-dreffer*, St. Auguftines-back.

Elliott, John, *Vinegar-maker*, 26, Hoft-street.

Elliott, John, *Carpenter*, Berkely-place.

Ellis, Nicholas, *Bright-smith*, Milk-street.

Ellis, John, *Bifcuit-baker*, 87, Caftle-street.

Ellis, Walter, *Bafket-maker*, Baldwin-street.

Ellifon, Mary, *Lodging-houfe*, Kingfdown-parade.

Ellifon, Richard and Co. *Wine and Brandy-merchants*, Old-market.

Elfworthy,

Elfworthy, William, *Pawnbroker*, Caftle-ditch.
Elton, William, *Merchant*, Clifton-hill.
Elton, Ames, and Co. *Gunpowder-office*, Exchange.
Elton, John, *Architect*, *Dolphin*, New-ftreet.
Elton, Miles, and Co. *Crown* and *Glass-bottle manufacturers*, Cheefe-lane, St. Philips,
Elton, William, *Merchant*, Bridge-parade.
Emblen, John, *Quill-manufacturer*, Redcliff-ftreet.
Embley, William, *Picture-frame maker*, Horfe-fair.
Emmett, Charles, *Three Sugar-loaves*, St. Michaels-steps.
Emmett, Sarah, *Golden Bowl*, Jacob-ftreet.
Emmy, Thomas, *Brandy-merchant*, Redcliff-hill.
Engledue, William, *Carpenter*, Pipe-lane.
Engledue, Capt. William, Ditto.
Enicell, Mary, *Staffordfhire-warehouse*, Back.
Errington, Richard, *Grocer*, Broad-ftreet.
Efcott, John Kirkpatrick, Gent. Montague-ftreet.
Efmand, Jofeph, *Bookbinder and Stationer*, John-ftreet.
Ettry, John, *Stay-maker*, Wine-ftreet.
Evans, John, *Lamb and Anchor*, Milk-ftreet.
Evans, David, Gent. 26, Queen-fquare.
Evans, H. F. *Stationer*, Back.
Evans, Neal, and Co. *Tobacconifts*, Ditto.
Evans, and Son, *Deal-merchants*, Ditto.
Evans, John, *Strap and Block*, Quay.
Evans, Evan, *Woollen-draper*, Corn-ftreet.
Evans, John and Co. *Woollen-drapers and Mens-mercers*, 23, Bridge-ftreet.
Evans, Ifrael, *Brick-maker*, Durdham-down.
Evans, William, *York Hotel*, Glocefter-place, Clifton.
Evans, Jofiah, *Florift*, Limekiln-lane.
Evans, Ann, *Grocer*, Ditto.
Evans, William, *Wine-merchant*, St. Michaels-hill.
Evans, William, *Liquor-merchant*, Paul-ftreet.
Evans, John, *Merchant*, 15, Ditto.
Evans, Ezekiel, *Carpenter*, Marlborough-ftreet.
Evans, Evan, *Glazier*, Horfe-fair.
Evans, James, *Mayor's-officer*, Kings-head-court.
Evans, John, *Corn-factor*, Chriftmas-ftreet.
Evans, John, *Currier*, 20, Weft-ftreet.
Evans, Margaret, *Bell*, St. James's-back.
Evans, Thomas, *Marquis of Granby*, Great Ann-street
Evans, Thomas Moore, *Cornfactor*, Thomas-ftreet.
Evans, Samuel, *Clothier*, Pennywell-lane.
Evans, Robert, *Cork-cutter*, 36, Redcliff-ftreet.

Evans

Evans, Evan, *Brick-maker*, Upper Eaſton.
Evans, William, *Yeoman*, Bedminſter.
Evans, William, *Deal-merchant*, Redland.
Evans, John, *Yeoman*, Durdham-down.
Evans, John, *Cabinet-maker*, Broad-mead.
Everett, Eleanor, *Ship*, Hanover-ſtreet.
Ewer, Mr. James, Dighton-ſtreet.

F

Fargus, John, *Auctioneer*, 3, Caſtle-ditch.
Farley, Thomas, *Salt-merchant*, Quay-head
Farmer, George, *Brightſmith*, Jacob-ſtreet.
Farquarſon, Capt. John, 13, St, Auguſtines-back.
Farr, William, *Conveyancer*, Montague-ſtreet.
Farr, John, *Working Silverſmith*, Tower-hill.
Farr, John, Eſq. *Alderman*, Redland.
Farrant, Francis, *Writing-maſter*, Broad-mead.
Fear, James, *Lodgings*, 4, Albemarle-row, & 1, Budge-row,
     Hotwells.
Fear, Samuel, *Tide Surveyor*, Alfred-place, Kingſdown.
Fear, William, *Carpenter*, Old-market.
Fear, John, *George*, Temple-ſtreet.
Fedden, William, *Sugar-refiner*, Counter-ſlip.
Felix, Capt, Dimond, King-ſtreet.
Felton, Mary, *Lodging-house*, 4, Hotwell-parade.
Felton, Thomas, *Butcher*, 12, St. Auguſtines-back.
Fenton, Thomas, *Watch-maker*, Ellbroad-ſtreet.
Ference, William, *Taylor*, Bridewell-lane.
Ferris, Thomas, *Shoemaker*, Quay.
Ferris, Robert, *Griffin Inn*, Griffin-lane.
Ferris, Robert, *White-hart*, Lower Maudlin-lane.
Ferry, John, *Lodging-house*, 4, Hotwell-parade.
Ferry, John, *Long-rooms*, Hotwells.
Fields, Capt William, Cannons-marſh.
Fiſher, Francis, *Merchant*, 31, Princes-ſtreet.
Fiſher, Duncan, *Ship-broker*, Quay.
Fiſher, John, *Deal-merchant*, 13, Trinity-ſtreet.
Fiſher, George, *Cheese-factor*, Temple-ſtreet
Fiſher, Francis, *Insurance-broker*, Exchange.
Fiſon, Joſeph, *Butcher*, Nicholas-ſtreet.
Fitchett, Thomas, *Salt-officer*, Charles's-ſtreet
Fitchew, Stephen and James, *Grocers*, Redcliff-hill.
Fitzhenry, Mr. Patrick, Durdham-down.

E   Flecy,

Flecy, Daniel, *Curriers-arms*, Queen-ftreet.
Fletcher, Thomas, *Tyler and Plaifterer*, Milk-ftreet.
Fletcher, James, *Cooper*, King-ftreet.
Fletcher, Ifaac, *Hair-dreffer*, 8, Caftle-ftreet.
Fletcher, George, *Tyler and Plaifterer*, Park.
Fletcher, Philip, *Grocer*, 3, North-ftreet.
Fletcher, William, *Tallow-chandler*, Weft-ftreet.
Fletcher, Robert, *Soap-maker and chandler*, 3, Old-market
Fletcher, William, *Accomptant*, Cathay.
Flook, John, *Hooper*, New-ftreet.
Flook, Job, jun *Cooper*, Lamb-ftreet.
Flook, Thomas, *Cooper*, Glocefter-lane.
Flower, Henry, *Pawnbroker*, Great Ann-ftreet.
Flower, Thomas, *Mafter of the City-school*, Hoft-ftreet.
Foley, Andrew, *Taylor*, Small-ftreet.
Fone, Thomas, *Pawnbroker*, 16, Hanover-ftreet.
Foot, George, *Coach-carver*, Brandon-ftreet.
Foot, William, *Maltfter*, Without Temple-gate.
Forafaffy, Amelia, *Ladies' Boarding-school*, Portland-ftreet.
Ford, William, *Cooper*, King-ftreet-hall.
Ford, Daniel, *Mason*, Lewins-mead.
Ford, Jonathan, *Black-horse*, Lawrence-hill.
Ford, Jofeph, *Hair-dreffer*, 147, Redcliff-ftreet.
Ford, James, *Wine-cooper*, Black-friers.
Ford, Mrs. H. F. Clifton.
Foreman, George, Gent. 3, Sion-hill,
Forfyth, Capt. Hammet, 20, Montague-ftreet.
Forth, James, *Confectioner*, Peter-ftreet.
Fofter, Weftcomb, *Merchant*, Lewins-mead.
Fothergill, and Sons, *Brafs-Founders, Coppersmiths, &c.* Redcliff-
Fowler, Henry, *Wire-drawer and worker*, Redcliff-ftreet.
Fowler, John, *Crab's-well*, Frog-lane.
Fowler, James, *Merchant*, Small-ftreet, & 7, Park-ftreet
Fownes, Mary, *Hooper*, Merchant-ftreet.
Fox, William, *Ship-chandler*, Princes-ftreet.
Fox, William, *Auctioneer*, Thunderbolt-ftreet.
Foxhall, Martin, *Carver and Gilder*, Hotwell-road.
Foxhill, Francis, *Butcher*, 7, North-ftreet.
Frampton, John, Gent. 21, King-fquare.
Francis, Ann and Son, *Undertakers*, Bridge-ftreet.
Francis, John, *Lodging-house*, Park.
Francis, John, *Accomptant*, Quakers-friers.
Franklin, George, and Co. *Tobacconifts*, Back.
Franklin, John, *Hair-dreffer*, 25, Montague-ftreet.
Franklin, Prudence, *Stay-maker*, Culver-ftreet.

Frappell

Frappell, William, *King's-arms*, Bedminster.
Frapwell. Thomas, *Tea-dealer*, 61, Wine-street.
Freeman, Miss, Clifton.
Freeman, John, and Copper Co *Copper-merchants*, Small-street.
Freeman, John, *Three horse-shoes*, Glocester-lane.
French, John, *Working Silversmith*, Tower-lane.
French, Arnold, *Pawnbroker*, Kings-head-court.
French, Thomas, *Nursery and Seedsman*, Lawrence-hill.
Freshwater, Samuel, *Excise-officer*, Park.
Fricker, George, *Accomptant*, Redcliff-hill
Fripp, Samuel, and Co. *Soap-manufacturers and chandlers*, 47, Castle-street.
Fripp, Mr. Samuel, jun. 16, Somerset-street.
Fripp, Mr. William, 22, Ditto.
Fromont, Edward and Co. *Flying-waggons*, Broad-mead.
Froome, Thomas, *Carpenter*, Berkely-place.
Frost, John, *Baker*, Thomas-street.
Frost, Richard, *Coach and Horses*, Redcliff-street.
Frost, William, *Baker*, Ditto.
Fry, John, *Hosier*, 9, High-street.
Fry, Robert, *Woollen-draper*, 30, Castle-street.
Fry, Peter, *Carpenter*, Upper Maudlin-lane.
Fry, Ebenezer, *Writing-master*, Charles's-street
Fry, Thomas, *Lampblack-manufacturer*, Elbroad-street.
Fry, Anna and Son, *Chocolate-makers*, 7, Union-street.
Fry, and Co. *Soap-manufacturers*, St. Philips-place.
Fry, William, *Distiller and Wine-merchant*, 104, Redcliff-street.
Fry, John, *Lodging-house*, Redland.
Fry, Capt. Richard, Little King-street.
Fryer, Mark, *Accomptant*, Jacob-street.
Fudge, John, *Mason*, Lawrence-hill.
Fugill, Joseph and Co. *Woollen-drapers*, Castle-street.
Furlong, Thomas, *Grocer*, Steep-street.
Furse, Philip, *Merchant*, 17, Queen-square.
Fuss, William, *Mariner*, College-street.
Fuss, Ann, *Butcher*, 4, Barton.
Fustell, John, *Roap-maker*, Lawrence-hill.

G

Gaby, William, *Taylor*, West-street.
Gadd and James, *Maltsters and Brewers*, Temple-backs.
Gadd, James, *Master of Colstons-school*, Temple-street.
Gadd, Joseph and Co. *Potters*, Counter-slip.
E 2

Gadd, Thomas, *Accomptant*, 44, Caftle-green.
Gadridge, Thomas, *Pawnbroker*, Hotwell-road.
Gage, James, *Glazier*, Lawrence-hill.
Gage, Daniel, *Glazier*, Lamb-ftreet.
Gains, William, *French Stay-maker*, St. James's-church-yard.
Gail, Capt. John, Pipe-lane.
Galliot, John, *Mariner*, 12, Trenchard-lane.
Gandy, Harry, *Conveyancer*, 28, Caftle-green.
Gardener, William, *Intelligence-office*, Bridge-ftreet.
Gardener, John, *Mariner*, Limekiln-lane.
Gardener, Mr. Joel, 29, Somerfet-ftreet.
Garmfton, William, *Hair-dreffer*, Bath-ftreet.
Garnet and Co. *Patent Wheel-manufactory*, Bifhops-park.
Garratt, Francis, *Tea-dealer*, 24, Eath-ftreet.
Garfed, James, *Merchant*, Southwell-ftreet.
Gattrell, William, *Accomptant*, Temple-backs.
Gautier, Ann, *French School for young Ladies*, Kingfdown.
Gav, George, *Ironmonger*, Bridge-ftreet.
Gay, Robert, Gent, 20, Somerfet-ftreet.
Gay, Richard, *White Lyon*, Temple-ftreet.
Gayner, William, *Broker*, Caftle-green, office Corn-ftreet.
Gayton, William, *Baker*, Milk-ftreet.
Gee, Charles, *Taylor*, Wade-ftreet.
Gee, George, Efq. Locks-mills.
Gee, Richard, *Shoemaker*, Redcliff-ftreet.
Gees and Dibbin, *Tobacconifts*, Ditto.
Gees and Dibbin, *Diftillers*, Ditto.
George, Stephen, *Butter-merchant*, Newfoundland-ftreet.
George, Philip, *Porter-brewer*, 36, Queen-fquare.
George, John, *Hofier and Glover*, 21, Clare-ftreet.
George, William, *Leather-dreffer*, 3, Dolphin-ftreet.
George, Richard, *Timber-merchant*, Cannons-marfh.
George, George, *Dealer in Spirits*, St. James's-back.
George, John, *Excife-officer*, Great Ann-ftreet.
George, William, *Umbrella-maker*, Broad-mead.
George, Philip and Co. *Porter-brewers*, Bath-ftreet.
Gething, Thomas, *Shopkeeper*, 3, Paul-ftreet.
Gibbons, William, and Co. *Merchants*, Princes-ftreet
Gibbons, Daniel, *Lodging-house*, 16, Paul-ftreet.
Gibbons, Martin, *Sadler*, Redcliff-ftreet
Gibbs, George, *Merchant*, Lodge-ftreet.
Gibfon, John, *Blue Pofts*, Temple-ftreet.
Gifford, Nathaniel, Efq. 12, King-fquare.
Gifford, and Eckley, *Manchefter-warehouse*, Bridge-ftreet
Gilbert, Capt. Robert, 13, Pipe-lane.

Gill,

Gill, Edward, *Merchant Taylor*, King-ftreet.
Gill, Elizabeth, *Shoemaker*, St. Auguftines-back.
Gillam, H. *Carpenter*, College-ftreet.
Gillam, George, *Accomptant*, 5, St James's-parade.
Gillard, Jofeph, *Roap-maker*, Thomas-ftreet.
Gillard, Robert, *Roap-maker*, Redcliff-ftreet.
Gingell, John, *Coach-mafter*, 2, Barton-ftreet.
Gingell, Thomas, *Hooper*, Broad-mead.
Glafcodine, Jofeph, *Carpenter and Mill-wright*, Stokes-croft.
Gode, Henry, Gent. Hotwells.
Godfrey, Mr. Henry, 60, St. Michaels-hill.
Godfrey, Henry, *Glazier*, Temple-ftreet.
Godwin, John, *Dealer in Earthen-ware*, Castle-green.
Gold, Edward, *Shoemaker*, Tower-hill.
Gold, James, *Hog-butcher*, Temple-street.
Goldney, Mrs. Ann, Clifton-hill.
Goldfworthy, James, *Roap and Twine-maker*, Thomas-street.
Goldfworthy, Robert, *Cabinet-maker*, Ditto.
Goldfworthy, Mary and Sons, *Roap, Twine and Sack-makers*, Without Temple-gate.
Gollege, William, *Mason*, Barrs-ftreet.
Gollege, Martha, *Crown*, Newgate-ftreet.
Gollifer,　　　　*Sadler*, Hotwell-road.
Gomond, Samuel, *Merchant*, 38, Princes-ftreet.
Goodridge, John, Efq. Great Georges-ftreet.
Goodridge, Capt. John, 11, Wells's-ftreet.
Gordon, Capt. James, York-ftreet.
Gordon, John, Efq. *Merchant*, Park-ftreet.
Gordon, John, *Merchant*, 2, Barton.
Gorton, William, *Turner and Chair-maker*, Old King-ftreet.
Gofley, Samuel, *Butcher*, New-ftreet
Gofs, John, *Accomptant*, 10, Newfoundland-ftreet.
Gofs, Andrew, *Butcher*, King-ftreet.
Gough, Abraham, *Cabinet-maker*, Horfe-fair.
Gough, Samuel and Thomas, *Millwrights*, Temple-ftreet,
Gough, Mary, *Haberdafher*, 49, Redcliff-ftreet.
Gower, John, *Mariner*, King-ftreet.
Gowing, George, *Moon and Stars*, Bedminfter.
Grace, Ifrael, *Chepftow Boat*, Back.
Grace, Ann, *Child-bed Linen-warehoufe*, Dolphin-ftreet.
Grace, Thomas, *Hallier*, Redcliff-backs.
Graham, James, *Surveyor of the Diftilleries*, Thomas-ftreet.
Grainger, Edward, *Surveyor of the Salt duties*, Cannon-ftreet,
Granger and Cropper, *Coopers*, King-ftreet.
Granger and Cropper, *Merchants*, Tontine-warehoufe, Quay.

　　　　　　　　　　　　　　　　　　　Granger,

Granger, Thomas, *Tripe-house*, St. James's-back.
Grant, John, *Accomptant*, 5, Newfoundland-street.
Grant, Robert, *Toy-maker*, Back-street.
Grant, George, *Butcher*, 7, Christmas-street,
Gravenor, William, *Sugar-refiner*, Brunswick-square.
Gravenor, St. Albyn, Ditto.
Gravenor, Mr. William, Upper Maudlin-lane.
Gravenor, William and Sons, *Sugar-refiners*, Rosemary-street.
Grave, Capt. William, College-street.
Graves, William, *Merchant*, Small-street.
Gray, Thomas and Co. *Pontypool-manufactory*, Temple-backs.
Grayall, William, *Shoemaker*, Hotwell-road.
Green, William, *Cabinet-maker*, Milk-street.
Green, John, *Cabinet-maker*, Princes-street.
Green, William, *Linen-draper*, Wine-street.
Green, Thomas, *Lodging-house*, Chapel-row.
Green and Barry, *Watch-makers*, Paradise-row.
Green, Mary, *Lodging-house*, Clifton-hill.
Green, Joseph, *Anchor*, Limekiln-lane.
Green, William, *Carpenter*, Upper Maudlin-lane
Green, Thomas, *Custom-house officer*, Portland-street.
Green, William, *Accomptant*, Dove-street.
Green, Joseph, *Accomptant*, Carolina-row.
Green, Sarah, *Circulating Library*, John-street.
Green, Samuel, *Plane-maker*, Cyder-house-passage.
Green, Samuel, *Academy for young Gentlemen*, Castle-green.
Green, Joseph, *Cutler*, Back-street.
Green, Ann, *Plume of Feathers*, Glocester-lane.
Green, William, Gent. Avon-street.
Green, Susannah, *Roap-maker*. Tower-street.
Greenway, John, *Star Inn*, Bedminster.
Greenwood, Benjamin, *British Tontine-office*, Maryport-street.
Greenwood, Benjamin, *Silk-dyer*, Christmas-street.
Greenwood, Edward, *Toy-warehouse*, Bridge-street.
Greenwood, Joseph, *Mariner*, Guinea-street.
Gregory, Sarah, *Marquis of Granby*, Baldwin-street.
Gresley, John, *Merchant*, 36, Queen-square.
Greethead, J. *Banker*, Corn-street.
Greville, Mr Francis, Park.
Griffin,   *Livery Stable-keeper*, Limekiln-lane.
Griffiths, Councellor,   Brunswick-square.
Grifiths, Edward, *Baker*, Milk-street.
Griffiths, William, *Anchorsmith*, 23, Princes-street.
Griffiths and Ludlow, *Linen-drapers*, Wine-street.
Griffith's *Anchor-manufactory*, College-street.

Griffith

Griffiths, John, *Cabinet-maker*, Horfe-fair.
Griffiths, William, *Three Crown Tavern*, St. Philips.
Grigg, Hull and Grigg, *Haberdafhers*, Briftol-bridge.
Grigg, Robert, Gent. Bedminfter-caufeway.
Grigg, Sufannah, *Jolly Sailor*, Bedminfter.
Grimes, Richard, *Academy for young gentlemen*, Hillgrove-ftreet.
Grimes, Dutton, *Mafter of the Boarding-fchool*, Durdham-down.
Grindon, Jofeph, *Tyler and Plaifterer*, 7, Culver-ftreet.
Grifley, Thomas, Gent. 1, Wells's-ftreet.
Grift, George, Gent. Clifton-hill.
Grove, Jofeph, *Butcher*, Hotwell-road.
Grove, Jofeph, *Cuftom-houfe officer*, Horfield-lane.
Grove, Sarah, *Gingerbread-baker*, Pennywell-lane.
Grove, Poutney and Richardfon, *Paper-makers*, Bridge-parade.
Grumley, Capt William, Park
Grummant, Ann, *Ladies' Boarding-fchool*, Queens-parade.
Gummer, John, *Cloth-bleecher*, Bedminfter.
Guppy and Armftrong, *Iron-mongers and Cutlers*, Back.
Gurner, James, *Briftol Tavern*, Small-ftreet.
Gurner, John, *Bear Inn*, St. Michaels-hill.
Gurner, James, *Berkely Caftle*, Berkely-fquare.
Gurney, Jofeph, *Watch-maker and Jeweller*, Corn-ftreet.
Guy, Henry, *Coach-mafter*, Limekiln-lane.
Guy, Jofeph, *Seminary for young gentlemen*, St. James's-parade.
Guy, Job, *Three Black-birds*, Stapleton-road.
Guy, Efau, *Tin-plate-worker*, Bath-ftreet.
Gwinnett, George, *Mealman*, 27, Old-market.
Gwyer, John, *Carpenter*, Newfoundland-ftreet.
Gwyer, Jofeph, *Accomptant*, 16, Princes-ftreet.
Gwyer, James, *Roap and Twine-maker*, Without Temple-gate.
Gwyer, John, *Umbrella-maker*, Bedminfter-caufeway.

H

Hack, Nicholas, *Nailer*, Glocefter-lane.
Hacket, Cornelius, *Stocking-manufacturer*, Wine-ftreet.
Haddock, Thomas, *Blackmoores-head*, Durdham-down.
Haghfton, John, Gent. Kingfdown.
Hagley, Fortunatus, *Taylor*, Orchard-ftreet.
Hague, Daniel, *Mason and Architect*, Wilder-ftreet.
Hague, Hill, Brice and Co. *Brick-makers*, Redclift-yard.
Hale, Richard and Thomas, *Braziers and Pewterers*, Back.
Hale, John, Efq 11, College ftreet.

Hale,

Hale, John, *Carpenter*, 8, Oxford-ftreet.
Hale, Henry, *Wine-merchant*, Redcrofs-ftreet.
Hale, Jofeph, *Tyler and Plaifterer*, Merchant-ftreet.
Hall, Robert, *Woollen-draper*, 40, High-ftreet.
Hall, Jofeph, *Grocer and Tea-dealer*, Maryport-ftreet.
Hall, Samuel and Co. *Wool-merchants*, Quay-ftreet.
Hall, John, Gent. 13, North-ftreet.
Hall, Capt. John, Dove-ftreet.
Hall, John, *Glazier*, Broad-mead.
Halftone, Thomas, *Turner*, Horfe-fair.
Haly, Peter, *Bookfeller*, Redcliff-ftreet.
Hamell, William, *Bell*, Quay-lane.
Hamilton, Capt. John, Stoney-hill.
Hamlen, Edward, *Dealer in Spirits*, St. Stephens-ftreet, and St
    Auguftines-back.
Hamley, William, *Mariner*, 63, Queen-fquare.
Hammond, Mary, *Currier*, Broad Ware.
Hancock, Philip, *Bright-fmith*, Back.
Hancock, Ifaac, *Clerk of St. Auguftines*, Lower-green.
Hancock, George, *Cheefe-factor*, St. Auguftines-back.
Hancock and Co. *Slate-merchants*, Ditto.
Hancock, John, *Livery Stable-keeper*, Kingfdown-parade.
Hancock, Mary, *Wheelwright*, Old-market.
Hankins, Thomas, *Heel and Laft-maker*, King-ftreet.
Hanmer, Thomas, *Wholefale Grocer*, Small-ftreet, and 10,
    Pipe-lane.
Hann, Robert, *Heel and Patten-maker*, Sims's-alley.
Hannett, George, *Hair-dreffer*, 29, Hillgrove-ftreet.
Hanfard, Providence, *Cornfactor and Seedfman*, Redcliff-ftreet
Hardiman, John, *Coach-mafter*, Frog-lane.
Hardiman, Richard, *Accomptant*, Montague-ftreet.
Harding, Sarah, *Butcher*, Hotwell-road.
Harding, J. *Taylor*, Lower College-ftreet.
Harding, Nathaniel, *Hooper*, Old-market.
Harding, Thomas, *Butcher*, St. James's-back.
Harding, William, Gent. Upper Eafton.
Harding and Tipton, *Diftillers*, Redcliff-ftreet.
Harding, I. H. *Kings-head*, Boot-lane, Bedminfter.
Hardwick, Samuel, *Baker*, Elbroad-ftreet.
Hardy, John, *Accomptant*, Bedminfter-caufeway
Hare, John, *Painter and Floor-cloth manufacturer*, King-ftreet.
Hare, William, fen. *Dancing-mafter*, Montague-ftreet.
Hare, William, jun. *Dancing-mafter*, Ditto.
Hare, Abraham, *Permit-writer*, Cherry-lane.
Harford, John Scandrett, Efq. *Banker*, Brunfwick-fquare.

Harford

Harford, John, *Mason*, Philadelphia-street,

Harford, Charles, *Merchant*, Princes-street.

Harford, James, *Merchant*, St. Auguftines-place.

Harford, Partridge, and Co. *Iron and Tin-plate merchants*, Small-ftreet.

Harford's and Briftol, *Braſs-company*, Ditto.

Harford's and Briftol, *Braſs-company*, Queen-ftreet.

Harford's and Briftol, *Brais and Copper-company*, Baptift-mills.

Harford, Charles, Efq. *Deputy Comptroler of the Cuftoms*, St. Michaels-hill.

Harford, Edward, Efq. 20, King-fquare.

Harford, Joſeph, Efq. 1, Dighton-ftreet.

Harford, James, *Iron-foundery-company*, Jacob-ftreet.

Harmer, Jeremiah, *Horn-worker*, Gloceſter-lane.

Harper, and Son, *Grocers*, 27, Caftle-ftreet.

Harper and Wolf, *Coach-makers*, Limekiln-lane.

Harris, Rees, *Taylor*, Penn-ftreet.

Harris, George, *Grocer*, 36, Caftle-ftreet.

Harris, John, *Mason*, 1, Sion-row, Clifton.

Harris, Prideaux, and Co. *Wine and Fruit-merchants*, Wine-ftr.

Harris, James, *Wine-merchant*, Unity-ftreet.

Harris, Haffelden, and Co. *Wholefale Grocers*, Quay-head.

Harris, Joſeph, *Cuftom-houfe officer*, Kington-buildings.

Harris, John, jun. *Sugar-refiner*, Montague-ftreet.

Harris, John, *Union*, Marlborough-ftreet.

Harris, John, Efq. *Alderman*, Stokes-croft.

Harris, John and Sons, *Sugar-refiners*, Lewins-mead.

Harris, Francis, *Merchant*, Ditto.

Harris and Savery, *Bankers*, Narrow Wine-ftreet.

Harris, Price, and Co. *Merchants*, Weft-ftreet.

Harris, Edward, *Grocer*, Back-ftreet.

Harris, Wintour, *Deputy Chamberlain*, Cathay.

Harris, Abraham, *Carpenter*, Beikely-fquare.

Hart, Hammet, *Dentift*, Avon-ftreet.

Hartland, William, *Carpenter*, Lower Maudlin-lane.

Harvey, Wafon, and Co. *Iron-mafters and merchants*, Quay

Harvey. James, Efq. Park-ftreet.

Harvey, Thomas, *Mariner*, 12, Hanover-ftreet.

Harwood, Richard, *Shoemaker*, 31, High-ftreet.

Harwood, James, *Linen-draper*, 15, Maryport-ftreet.

Haſkins, James, *Brightfmith*, Whitfun-court.

Haſkins, Samuel, *Grocer*, Kingſdown.

Haſkins, Parſons, *Broker*, Thomas-ftreet.

Haffell, John, *Accomptant*, Rack-cloſe.

Hawker, George, *Lodging-houfe*, Montague-ftreet.

F

Hawkes,

Hawkes, James, *Taylor*, North-ftreet, Bedminfter.
Hawkefwell, Richard, Efq. *Chamberlain*, Charles's-ftreet.
Hawkins and Co. *Woollen-drapers and Wine-merchants*, High-ftr.
Hawkins, William, *Waggon and Horfes*, Peter-ftreet.
Hawkins, Charles, *Sadler*, St. Auguftines-back.
Hawkins, Capt. William, Park.
Hawkins, William, *Three Tuns*, Lawrence-hill.
Hawkins, William, *Baker*, Glocefter-lane.
Hawkins, Robert, *Conveyancer*, High-ftreet.
Haworth, John, *Linen-draper*, 34, Ditto.
Haydon, Daniel, *Tallow-chandler*, Redcliff-ftreet.
Hayes, William, *Carpenter*, Dove-ftreet.
Hayes, Richard, *Gardener*, Lawrence-hill.
Hayes, William, *Hair-dreffer*, Quay.
Hayhurft, E. and M. *Corn and Flour-factors*, Bedminfter.
Haynes, William, *Mafter of Colftons-fchool*, St. Auguftines-place
Haynes, William, *Cabinet-maker*, Park.
Haynes, Richard and Thomas, *Iron-merchants*, Caftle-green.
Haynes, William, *Three Compaffes*, Jacob-ftreet.
Haynes, Thomas, *Hog-butcher*, Bedminfter-caufeway,
Haythorn, Jofeph, *Undertaker*, 40, High-ftreet.
Haythorn, Jofeph, *Leather-dreffer*, Broad Ware.
Hayward, Richard, *Ship-block-maker*, Queen-fquare.
Hazard, Catharine, *Plumber*, 29, Lewins-mead.
Hazard, Samuel, *Wheelwright*, Avon-ftreet, St. Philips.
Hazell, Either, *Seed-fhop*, Peter-ftreet.
Hazell, William, Gent. Caftle-green.
Hazell, Thomas, *Confectioner*, Without Temple-gate.
Headford, Robert, *Dealer in Spirits*, Caftle-ftreet.
Heard, William, *Gun-maker*, Redcliff-ftreet.
Heath and Grace, *Corn and Flour-factors*, 28, Caftle-ftreet.
Hebberd, John, *Plaifterer*, Stokes-croft.
Hedges, Thomas, *Hatter and Furrier*, 46, Caftle-ftreet.
Hedges, Ann, *Blackmoores-head*, Lamb-ftreet.
Heffer, Henry, *Baker*, Little Ann-ftreet.
Heighington, Mary, *Confectioner*, St. Michaels-hill.
Hellicar, Ames and Sons, *Merchants*, Queen-fquare.
Helps, William, *Merchant*, Ditto.
Hemmett, Edward, *Butcher*, New-ftreet.
Hemming, Thomas, *Hallier*, under the Bank.
Hemming, Thomas, *Pawnbroker*, Lower Maudlin-lane.
Hemming, John, *Needle and Fyfh-hook-maker*, Jack of Newbery,
    St. James's-back.
Henbury, William, *Cooper*, Kingfdown-parade.
- Henderfon, Thomas, *Taylor*, Quay.

Henderfon.

Henderfon, John, *Cuftom-houfe officer*, Kingfdown.
Henderfon, Samuel, *Merchant*, Barton.
Henderfon, Samuel and Co. *Sugar-refiners*, Halliers-lane.
Henep, William, *Glazier*, College-green.
Henley, William, *Collar and Harnefs-maker*, Hoft-ftreet.
Henley, William, *Accomptant*, Cathay.
Henley, Thomas, *Cuftom-houfe officer*, Lower-green.
Henfley, Capt. Chriftopher, Orchard-ftreet.
Henwood, Luke, *Architect*, 34, College-ftreet.
Herapath, Elizabeth, *Jolly Meeter*, Queen-ftreet.
Herapath, William, *Horfe and Jockey*, Marybufh-lane.
Herbert, R. M. *Wool-ftapler*, Bedminfter.
Herbert, Edward, *Wool-ftapler*, Ditto.
Herington, Lieut. Conway, Stoney-hill.
Hern, John, *Butcher*, Hotwell-road.
Hett, John, Efq. Clifton-hill
Hewlett, James, *French Stay-maker*, 39, Bridge-ftreet, and 31,
    High-ftreet.
Hewlett, John, *Brick-maker*, Upper Eafton.
Hewfon, John, *Lodging-houfe*, Hotwell-parade.
Hibbard, Sarah, *Maltfter*, Newfoundland-ftreet.
Hibbert, Richard, *Taylor*, 16, Guinea-ftreet.
Hibbs, William, Efq. Clifton.
Hickcocks, Robert, *Shoemaker*, Milk-ftreet.
Hickes, Daniel and Son, *Wine-hoopers*, Quay-ftreet.
Hickes, James, *Ship*, Steep-ftreet.
Hickes and Sevier, *Shoemakers*, 54, Redcliff-ftreet.
Hickes, William, *Writing-mafter*, Bedminfter.
Higgs, William, *Hat-maker*, Milk-ftreet.
Higgs, William, *Book-keeper*, Rack-clofe.
Highatt, Richard, Efq. Redcliff-parade.
Higgins, John, *Pawnbroker*, Milk-ftreet.
Higgins, Robert, *Bright-fmith*, Merchant-ftreet.
Hill, James, *Linen-merchant*, Union-ftreet.
Hill, Jeremiah, jun. Clifton-hill.
Hill, Jeremiah and Sons, *Merchants*, St. Stephen-ftreet.
Hill, William, *Tyler and Plaifterer*, Griffin-lane.
Hill, Edward, *Accomptant*, 23, Montague-ftreet.
Hill, Jofeph, *Carpenter*, Marlborough-ftreet.
Hill, James, *Umbrella-maker*, St James's church-yard.
Hill and Thompfon, *Glaziers*, Bridewell-lane.
Hill, Jonas, *Brass-founder*, 10, John-ftreet.
Hill, Mary and Son, *Hoopers*, Caftle-green.
Hill, John, *Tanner*, Elbroad-ftreet.
Hill, Benjamin, *Plumber*, Baldwin-ftreet.

Hill,

Hill, John, *Saracens-head*, Without Temple-gate.
Hill, James, *Rising Sun*, Temple-ftreet.
Hill, Jofiah, Gent. North-ftreet, Bedminfter.
Hillhoufe, James Martin, *Ship-builder*, Hotwell-road.
Hillhoufe, Mifs E. Horfield-lane.
Hillier, Thomas, *Wool-ftapler*, Caftle-ditch.
Hillier, James, *Taylor*, Redcliff-hill.
Hillman, Robert, *Wheelwright*, Bedminfter.
Hillyard, John, *Lodging-houfe*, Hotwell-road.
Hingfton, J. *Carpenter*, 6, North-ftreet.
Hinton, Jofeph, *Sadler*, Peter-ftreet, and 90, Redcliff-ftreet.
Hippefly, William, Efq. Clifton.
Hitchens, Mary, *Hat-maker*, Thomas-ftreet.
Hoare, Jofeph, *Cooper's-arms*, King-ftreet.
Hoare, James, *Callenderer and Glazer*, Broad-mead.
Hobbs, Capt. Daniel, 45, Princes-ftreet.
Hobbs, Mr. Thomas, Great Georges-ftreet.
Hobbs, John, *Cork-cutter*, Thomas-ftreet.
Hobbs, Jonathan, *Tin-plate-worker*, Ditto.
Hobbs, Thomas, *Houfe and Sign-painter*, Redcliff-ftreet.
Hodder, John, *Grocer*, 7, Chapel-row.
Hodder, Hefter, *Glafs-houfe*, Cheefe-lane.
Hodder, Benjamin, *Hair-dreffer*, Thomas-ftreet.
Hodge, Thomas. *Three Queen's Inn*, Thomas-ftreet.
Hodges, Sarah, *Baker*, Redcliff-hill.
Hodgfon, George, Gent. Cathay.
Hodgfon, Capt. Thomas, Wapping.
Holbrook, Sarah, *Haberdafher*, 36, Old-market.
Holbrook, Jofeph, *Glazier*, Bedminfter.
Holbrook, Thomas, *Brightfmith*, Ditto.
Holder, William, *Tobacco-merchant*, 17, Corn-ftreet.
Holdway, Robert, *Shoemaker*, Frog-lane.
Hole, William, Efq. Park-row.
Holiday, Mary, *Pawnbroker*, Cannon-ftreet.
Holiday, John, *Horn-worker*, Narrow Wine-ftreet.
Holland, Jarvis, Peter and George, *Starch, Fig-blue, and Orchil*
 marufacturers, Broad-mead.
Holland, Peter, *Merchant*, King-fquare.
Holland, John, *Hare and Hounds*, Temple-ftreet.
Hollandfworth, John, *Accomptant*, College-ftreet.
Hollis, E. *Lodging-houfe*, Clifton.
Hollifter, Lawrence, *Cuftom-houfe officer*, Park.
Holman, William, *Leopard*, Frog-lane.
Holman, James, *Miller*, Newgate-ftreet.
Holmes, Capt. Eufibia, 7, Norfolk-ftreet.

Holmes

Holmes, Charles, *Ship block-maker*, Quay.
Holmes, Thomas, *Wharfinger*, Quay-head.
Home, Miss, *Ladies' Boarding-school*, College-green.
Homyard, John, *Bellows-maker*, Bedminster.
Honeychurch, Thomas, *Accomptant*, St. Philips.
Honnywell, Capt. Richard, 15, Trinity-street.
Hook, John, *Butcher*, Montague-street.
Hookway, James, *Horse and Jockey*, Thomas-street.
Hooper, James, *Mason*, Hotwell-road.
Hooper, John, *Hallier*, Limekiln-lane.
Hooper, Henry, *Accomptant*, 1, Somerset-street.
Hooper, James, *Painter*, 36, Stokes-croft.
Hooper, Mary, *Ship*, Old-market.
Hooper, William, *Maltster*, Ditto.
Hooper, Thomas, *Maltster*, Ditto.
Hooper, Richard, *Mariner*, 9, Somerset-square.
Hope, John, *Potter*, Temple-street.
Hopkins, Hannah, *Shakespeare*, Princes-street.
Hopkins, Watkin, *Hooper*, 72, Stokes-croft.
Hopkins, Ralph, *Wholesale Bacon-dealer*, Old-market.
Hopkins, John, *Carpenter*, Thomas-street.
Hopkins, Jane, *Stag and Hounds*, Merchant-street.
Hopton, Ann, *Brush-maker*, Maryport-street.
Horler, Joseph, *Cutler*, Bridewell-lane.
Horler, Joseph, *Mayor's-officer*, 2, Norfolk-street.
Horne, William, *Carpenter*, Lower College-street.
Horsley, Stephen, *Accomptant*, Horfield-lane.
Horwood, William, *Butcher*, Milk-street.
Hosey, John, *Shoemaker*, Lower College-street.
Hoskins, George, *Painter*, Hotwell-road.
Hoskins, Richard, *Working Silversmith*, John-street.
Hoskins, *Stay-maker*, Ditto.
Houlson, Robert, *Shoemaker*, Cannons-marsh.
Houlton, Gracious, *Cabinet-maker*, Wilder-street.
Hounsell, Thomas, *Grocer*, Redcliff-street.
Housden, Mr. Daniel, Rosemary-street.
House, William, *Farrier*, Old King-street.
House, George, *Biscuit-baker*, Rosemary-street.
House, David, *Dealer in Spirits*, Temple-street.
House, Hannah, *Dealer in Spirits*, Redcliff-street.
Houston, John, *Broker*, Pithay.
How, John, *Confectioner*, Corn street.
How, Mrs. Elizabeth, 13, Stokes-croft
Howard, William, *Hair-dresser*, Redcliff-hill.
Howard, Capt. Benjamin, 4, Kingtons-buildings.

Howe,

Howe, Robert, *Silversmith, Cutler and Jeweller*, Clare-street.
Howell, Thomas, *Music-seller*, 12, Ditto.
Howell, William, *Linen-draper*, Bridge-street.
Howell, Capt. Devereux, St. Augustines-place.
Howell, Benjamin, *Fox*, Horse-fair.
Howell, Joseph, *Cheese-factor*, Temple-street.
Howland, Thomas, *Carpenter*, Newfoundland-street.
Huberfeld, Joseph, *Fox*, Redcliff-street.
Hudson, John, *Mariner*, Dove-street.
Hughes, Wells, and Co. *Linen-drapers*, Wine-street.
Hughes, Benjamin, *Linen-draper*, Union-street.
Hughes, Joseph, *Linen-draper*, Castle-street.
Hughes, Joseph, Gent. Cathay.
Hughes, Jane, *Lodging-house*, Durdham-down.
Hughes, John, *Secretary to the Bristol Fire-office*, Hillgrove-street
Hughes, Joseph, *Late Groom to his Grace the Duke of Portland*
    Masons-arms, St. James's-street.
Huish, John, *Tyler and Plaisterer*, White-friers
Hulbert, Ester, *Butcher*, Butcher-row,
Hull, William, *Brandy-merchant*, Montague-street.
Hull, Thomas, *Custom-house officer*, 4, Cathay.
Hull, John, *Haberdasher*, 9, Somerset-street.
Hull, John, *Smith*, Temple-street.
Humphries, Ann, *Plume of Feathers*, Hotwell-road.
Humphries, William, *Sheriffs-officer*, Cannon-street
Humphries, John, *Patten-ring maker*, Stokes-croft.
Humphries, William, *Hair-dresser*, Host-street.
Humphries, Elijah, *Three Tuns*, Lawrence-hill.
Humphries, John, *Ironmonger*, Baldwin-street.
Humphries, Evan, *Duke of Devonshire*, Temple-street.
Humphries, Rogers, and Co. *Brewers*, Bath-street.
Hunt, Capt. Ashfield, 30, Princes-street
Hunt, John, *Cutler*, Quay.
Hunt, Anthony, *Cabinet-maker*, 28, Bridge-street.
Hunt, William, *Taylor and Salesman*, Union-street.
Hunt, William, *Brandy-merchant*, Dove-street.
Hunt, William, Gent. Old-market.
Hunt, Henry, *Cornfactor and Mealman*, 7, West-street.
Hunt, William, *Rose*, Thomas-street.
Hunter, M. H. and R. *Merchants*, Queen-square
Huntley, William, *Block-maker*, 26, Princes-street.
Huntingdon, Samuel, *Basket-maker*, Pithay.
Hurle, John, *Merchant*, Church-lane, St. Michaels.
Hurley, Richard, *Shoemaker*, 29, Clare-street.
Hurley, William, *Poulterer*, Baldwin-street.

Huston,

Huston, William, *Printer*, Castle-green.
Hutchins, Robert, *Merchant*, Kingsdown-parade.
Hutchins, Brice, and Co. *Brick-makers*, St. Philips.
Huxtable, George, *Grocer*, St. Nicholas-steps.

I

Ibberson, Benjamin, *Writing-master and Accomptant*, Castle-green.
Ile, Thomas, *Three Crowns*, Broad Ware.
Iles, Robert, *Baker*, Lewins-mead.
Iles, James, *Grocer*, Lawrence-hill.
Illing, Susannah, *Upholder*, Hillgrove-street.
Ingram, James, *Sugar-refiner*, St. Johns-bridge.
Inman, Thomas, *Pawnbroker*, Ditto.
Inman, Francis, *Stationer*, Quay-street.
Inman, Susannah, *Punch-house*, Redcliff-backs.
Ireland and Wright, *Wine and Brandy-merchants*, under the Bank.
Ireland, Wright, and Co. *Sugar-refiners*, Ditto.
Insh, John, *West-India Coffee-house*, Market-place.
Irons, Richard, *Butcher*, Newfoundland-street.
Isaacs, Samuel, *Butcher*, Redcliff-street.
Ivyleafe, Richard, Esq. 15, King-square.
Jacks, Thomas, *Taylor*, Philadelphia-street.
Jacks, Walter, *Merchant*, 33, Bridge-street, and 27, Somerset-
    street.
Jacks, Martin, *Custom-house officer*, Duke-street.
Jacks, Mr. Selby, Bedminster.
Jackson, Ann, *Lodging-house*, King-street.
Jackson, Joseph, *Bookbinder*, Lower Maudlin-lane.
Jackson, Richard, *Wine and Brandy-merchant*, Wilder-street.
Jackson, William, *Baker*, 37, Old-market.
Jackson, William, *Baker and Mealman*, St. Philips.
Jackson, Thomas, *Salt-refiner*, Redcliff-street.
Jackson, Samuel, *Accomptant*, Merchant-street.
Jacobs, Isaac, *Hair-dresser*, Quay.
Jacobs, Lazarus, *Glass-merchant*, Avon-street.
James, William, *Tyler and Plaisterer*, Milk-street.
James, George, and Co. *Hop and Brandy merchants*, King-street.
James, William, *Broker*, All-saints-lane.
James, Mary, *Stationer*, 3, Peter-street.
James, E. *Milliner and Haberdasher*, 88, Castle-street.
James, John, *Wine-merchant*, Dowry-square.
James, William, *Deal-merchant*, Hope-square.
James, Francis, *Shipwright*, Hotwell-road.

James,

James, John, *Taylor*, Marlborough-street.
James, Isaac, *Undertaker*, Circulating-library, North-street.
James, William, *Timber-merchant*, Limekiln-dock.
James, Nathaniel, *Sadler*, St. Michaels-hill.
James, Robert, *Cabinet-maker*, Terill-street.
James, George, *Carpenter*, St. James's church-yard.
James, William, *Hair-dresser*, Bridewell-lane.
James, Richard, *Rising Sun*, Castle-ditch.
James, John, *Carrier*, Lawrence-hill.
James, Samuel, sen. *Pawnbroker*, St. Philips-plain.
James, Samuel, jun. *Pawnbroker*, Ditto
James, Robert, *Heart and Crown*, Prince Eugean-lane.
James, Mary and Son, *Sadlers and Patent Trufs-makers*, 1\
    Redcliff-street.
James, Thomas, Gent. 25, Guinea-street.
James, Stephen, *Carpenter*, Bedminster-causeway.
Jameson, James, *Cabinet-maker*, Frog-lane.
James, Mary, *Three Boar's-heads*, Horse-fair.
Janes, H. and A. *Haberdashers*, Redcliff-street.
Jappie, Daniel, Gent. 4, Somerset-square.
Jarman, William, *Writing-master*, Rosemary-street
Jarrett, John, *Hop-merchant and Grocer*, Maryport-street.
Jarrett, William, *Grocer*, Union-street.
Jayne, John, *Yeoman*, 33, College-street.
Jayne, Richard, *Butcher*, St. Philips-plain.
Jaynes, John, *Cabinet-maker*, Park.
Jeff, Edward, *Plumber*, Merchant-street.
Jefferies, William, Gent. Trenchard-lane.
Jefferies, Abraham, *Corn-chandler*, Lamb-street.
Jefferies, Joseph, *Corn-chandler*, Christmas-street.
Jeffery and Serle, *Milliners and Haberdashers*, Old-market
Jeffery, Ariel, and Co. *Hat-manufacturers*, Wine-street.
Jeffery, John, *Catler and Hardwareman*, 2, Corn-street.
Jellett, William, *Brewer*, Lawrence-hill.
Jellott, William, *Three Cups and Salmon*, Redcliff-hill
Jenkins, Mary, *Lodging-house*, 4, Queen-square.
Jenkins, William, *Cheese and Butter-factor*, Maryport-street
Jenkins, Walter, *Broker and Auctioneer*, 21, Bridge-street.
Jenkins, Samuel, *Cork-cutter*, 38, Castle-street.
Jenkins, Capt. William, Barts.
Jenkins, George, *Mariner*, St. Augustines-back.
Jenkins and Lovell, *Carpenters*, Frog-lane.
Jenkins, Joseph, *Linen-draper*, 8, Carolina-row
Jenkins, Thomas, *Shoemaker*, Castle-ditch
Jenkins, Thomas, *Writing-master*, Redcross-street.

Jenkins, Thomas, *Carpenter*, Temple-street.
Jenkins, Lewis, *Red Lion*, Redcliff-street.
Jenkins, William, *Carpenter*, Broad-mead.
Jennings, James, *Taylor*, Pile-street.
Jennings, Francis, *Lodging-house*, Hotwells.
Jerman, William, *Excise-officer*, Redcross-street.
Jerritt, John, *Cabinet-maker*, Old King-street.
Jiffs, Gabriel, *Hair-dresser*, Horse-fair
Joce, Thomas, *Hair-dresser*, Clifton-hill.
Joce, Capt. Timothy, 12, Trinity-street.
Johnson, George, *Mason*, Penn-street.
Johnson, John, *Coach-maker*, Hotwell-road.
Johnson, James, *Tin-plate worker*, St. Augustines-back
Johnson, William, *Neptune*, Tucker-street.
Johnson, Sarah, *Dealer in Spirits*, Lawrence-hill
Johnson, George, *Rising Sun*, Temple-street.
Jolley, Alexander, *Perfumer*, Hotwells.
Jolley, Capt. James, 18, College-street.
Jolliff, William, *Landing-waiter*, Orchard-street.
Jones, George Spring, *Accomptant*, 8, Norfolk street
Jones, Jane, *Crown and Cushion*, Milk-street.
Jones, Thomas, *Livery Stable-keeper*, Leek-lane
Jones, and Son, *Millwrights*, Philadelphia-street.
Jones, Philip, *Merchant*, Queen-square.
Jones, Rebecca, *Staffordshire-warehouse*, Back.
Jones, Sarah, *Lodging-house*, 13, King-street.
Jones, John, *Trunk-maker*, Corn-street.
Jones, Richard, *Distiller*, Broad-street.
Jones, Abraham, *Shoemaker*, Maryport-street
Jones, Thomas, *Brush-maker*, Ditto.
Jones, Edward, *Sadle, and Bridle-cutter*, Peter-street.
Jones, Charles, *Butcher*, 17, Castle-street.
Jones, Elizabeth, *Haberdasher*, 41, Ditto.
Jones, William, *Lodgings*, 5 and 6, Sion-row, and 8, Glocester-
place, Clifton.
Jones, William, *Watch-maker*, Hotwell-road.
Jones, William, *Black-horse*, Ditto
Jones, Henry, *Mason*, 16, Denmark-street.
Jones and Billings, *Chimney-piece, and Composition ornament-manu-
facturers*, St Augustines-back
Jones, Dunn and Drewett, *Marble-masons*, under the Bank.
Jones, Henry, *Grocer*, 48, St. Michaels-hill.
Jones, William, *Taylor*, 53, Ditto
Jones, William, *Carpenter*, Ditto.
Jones, J. R. *Hair-dresser*, Ditto.

G

Jones,

Jones, Samuel, *Gardener*, Ditto.
Jones, David, *Hair-dresser*, Park.
Jones, Mr. Edward, Portland-street.
Jones, John, *Custom-house officer*, Ditto.
Jones, Thomas, *Accomptant*, 31, Montague-street.
Jones, James, *Taylor*, Charles's-street.
Jones, Thomas, *Pastry-cook*, 22, Ditto.
Jones, Thomas, *Merchant*, Barton-street.
Jones, Thomas, *Hooper*, Wilder-street.
Jones, Mr. William, 7, Dighton-street
Jones, George, *Plaisterer and Painter*, Daltons-court
Jones, James, *Horse-jockey and Farrier*, Square-lane
Jones, Edward, *Baker*, 27, Stokes-croft.
Jones, Richard, *Taylor*, 93, Ditto.
Jones, Mrs. Harriot, Host-street
Jones, William, *Malster and Brewer*, Redcross-street.
Jones, W. H. *Brush and Sieve-maker*, Nicholas-street, and Baldwin-street
Jones, Henry and Son, *Maltsters*, Glocester-lane.
Jones, James, *Merchant*, Penrywell-lane
Jones, John, *Excise-officer*, St. Philips.
Jones, David *Export Surveyor*, Cheese-lane.
Jones, David, *Shoemaker*, Thomas-street.
Jones, Mary, *Grocer*, Ditto
Jones, William, *Mason*, Temple-street.
Jones, Elizabeth, *Crown*, Prince Eugean-lane.
Jones, William, *Currier*, 49, Redcliff-street.
Jones, William, *Excise-officer*, Cathay.
Jones, William, *Boars-head*, Bedminster-causeway.
Jones, Felix, *Mason*, Redcliff church-yard.
Jones, Mr Charles, Durdham-down,
Jones, David, *Ship*, Broad-mead.
Jordan, John, *Mason*, 2, Paul-street.
Jordan, William, *Brazier*, Host-street.
Jordan, William, *Hooper*, Ditto
Jordan, Daniel, *Pine apple*, Limekiln-lane
Jorden and Jackson, *Mantua-makers*, College-street.
Joyce, James, *Bacon-merchant*, Cutlers-mills.

K

Kale and Tripp, *Maltsters*, St Philips-place.
Kater John and Henry, *Sugar-refiners*, Tucker-street.
Keeler, Robert, *Taylor*, Rosemary-street.

Keene, Thomas, *Sugar-refiner*, Redcliff-ftreet.
Keiquin, Thomas, *Corn-factor*, Exchange.
Kelly, Thomas, *Shoe-maker*, Broad-ftreet.
Kemis, Capt. James, Kingfdown-parade.
Kemis, Charles, *Accomptant*, Charles's-ftreet.
Kempfter, John, *Taylor*, St. Stephen-ftreet.
Kendall, James, *Plane-maker*, Pithay.
Kenfield, T. *Timber-dealer*, Bell, Back.
Kenney, Vincent, *Supervisor*, St. Philips.
Kerby, Mr. George, Park
Kerby and Beer, *Tea-dealers*, 13, Broad-ftreet.
Kerr, Capt. Charles, 5, Gay-ftreet.
Kettle, Elizabeth, *Tallow-chandler*, St. James's-back.
Keyes and Taylor, *Carpenters*, Limekiln-lane.
Kiddell, George, *Merchant*, Duke-ftreet
Kift, Thomas, *Infurance-broker*, Montague-ftreet, office, Church-
    lane, St Stephen's.
Kimber, Capt John, 27, Redcrofs-ftreet
Kimberly, Stephen, *Mufic-mafter*, Dove-ftreet.
Kimberly, John, *Sack-maker*, Temple-ftreet.
Kindon, John, *Broker and Auctioneer*, Peter-ftreet.
Kindon, Samuel, *Butcher*, Nicholas-ftreet.
Kindon, John, *Broker*, Thomas-ftreet.
King, Henry, *Sadlers' Ironmonger*, St Auguftines-back.
King, John and Son, *Cheese-factors*, Quay-head.
King, William, *Accomptant*, Dove-ftreet.
King, Benjamin, Gent. 88 Stokes-croft
King, Robert, *Glover and Undertaker*, John-ftreet.
King, Heath, and Co. *Hat-manufacturers*, Caftle-green.
King, Paul, *Accomptant*, 36, Ditto
King, Benjamin, *Cabinet-maker*, Old-market.
Kington, Thomas, Efq. Rodney-place, Clifton.
Kington, Edward, Gent Kingfdown-parade.
Kington, William, *Maltfter and Brewer*, Cathay.
Kirby and Howell, *Lampblack-manufacturers*, Bedminfter.
Kneath, Thomas, *Excife-officer*, 8, Caftle-ftreet.
Knight, John, *Merchant*, St. Auguftines-place.
Knight, Elizabeth, *Grocer*, Temple-ftreet.
Knox, George, *Black-horfe*, Lower-green.

L

Lacey, John, *Plaifterer and Painter*, Limekiln-lane
Lacey, William, *Tea-dealer*, St Michaels-hill.
Lacey,

Lacey, Samuel, *Crown*, Great-gardens.
Lacey, Paul, *Watch-maker*, All-faints-lane.
Lageman, William, *Merchant*, 16, St. Auguftines-back.
Lageman, Mrs.   *Milliner*, Ditto.
Lambden, Henry and Co. *Pin-manufacturers*, Jacob-ftreet.
Lambert, Francis, *Star*, under the Bank.
Lane, William, *Grocer*, Redcliff-ftreet.
Lane, Henry, *Watch-maker*, Quay.
Lane, Thomas, *Taylor*, Bedminfter.
Lane, Samuel, *Accomptant*, Baptift-mills.
Langdon,   *Sadler*, 6, College-ftreet.
Langdon, Capt. John, Culver-ftreet.
Langford, John, *Mariner*, Bloomfbury-buildings.
Langford, Robert, *Accomptant*, Marlborough-mount
Langley, Capt. John, 7, Jamaica-ftreet.
Langley, Sarah, *Wharfinger*, Back.
Lanfdown, Jofeph, *Bookbinder*, Tower-hill.
Lanfdown, William, *King's-head*, Stokes-croft.
Lanfdown, Jofeph, Gent Mortague-ftreet.
Langfhaw, William, *Cabinet-maker*, Milk-ftreet.
Langweil, Thomas, *Mason*, Ditto
Larkworthy, John, Gent. Trenchard-lane.
Larouche, Sir James, Bart. College-green.
Larwill and Stephens's *Equitable and Univerfal Tontine-office*,
    Mary-port-ftreet.
Latchmore, Nicholas, Gent. Milk-ftreet.
Latham, Mofely, *Newsman*, 6, College-green.
Lather, Sarah, *Ledging-houfe*, Stoney-hill
Lauder, Hugh, *Intelligence-office*, under the Bank
Lauder, Alexander, *Nurfery-man*, Stokes-croft
Lauder, Peter, *Nurfery and Seedsman*, Lawrence-hill.
Lavington, William, *Yeoman*, Portland-ftreet
Lawley, Andrew, *Brass and Wood Clock-maker*, Redcliff-ftreet
Lawley and Co. *Pork-butchers*,   Ditto.
Lawrence and Co *Shoe and Saddle-warehouse*, Ditto.
Lawrence, Stephen, *Butcher*, Caftle-ditch.
Lawrence, Anthony, *Annutto-manufacturer*, Stokes-croft.
Lawrence, Richard, *Lodging-houfe*, 35, College-ftreet
Lawrence, John, *Whip-mafter*, Newfoundland-ftreet.
Lawfon, Robert, *Baker*, 42, Caftle-ftreet.
Lawfon, Fry, Frampton, and Co *Glass-bottle manufacturers*,
    Cheefe-lane, St. Philips
Laxton, Mrs *Lodging-houfe*, Trinity-ftreet.   ·
Leach, Mary, *Three Compaffes*, Pithay
Leach, Joan and Co *Woollen-manuf. Grocers*, Queen-ftreet
                                    Leake,

Leakey, Thomas, *Salutation*, St. Philips-plain.
Lean, John, *Linen-merchant*, Unity-ftreet, Warehoufe in Wine-
    ftreet.
Leary, Matthew, *Carpenter*, Lower College-ftreet.
Ledgenham, Hefter, *Lodging-houfe*, Hotwells.
Lediard, Philip, *Linen-draper*, 13, Caftle-ftreet.
Lediard, Philip, *Dry-falter*, Temple-ftreet.
Lee, Rev. Charles, *Mafter of the City Grammar-school*, Unity-ftr.
Lee, John, *Butcher*, Nicholas-ftreet.
Lee, John, *Bell Inn*, Thomas-ftreet.
Lee, William, *Taylor and Habit-maker*, Durdham-down.
Leigh, William, *Yeoman*, Frefhford-alley.
Leigh, Thomas, *Maltfter*, Guinea-ftreet.
Leman, Thomas Curtis, Efq. Unity-ftreet.
Leman, Clement, *Accomptant*, Hillgrove-ftreet.
Leman, and Son, *Carding-machine manufaƈtory*, St. Philips.
Lendy, Capt. Robert, Back.
Lennot, Rebecca, *Maltfter*, Stapleton-road.
Leonard, Solomon, *Roap-maker*, Back.
Leonard, Elizabeth, *Lodging-houfe*, 20, King-ftreet.
Leonard and Co. *Cheese and Butter-faƈtors*, Maryport-ftreet.
Leonard, Daniel, *Lodging-houfe*, Hotwell-parade.
Leonard, Solomon, *Maltfter*, Lawrence-hill.
Leonard, John, *Queen's Head*, Broad-plain.
Leonard, Paul, *Edge-Tool maker*, Bedminfter.
Levy, H and L. *Opticians*, Temple-ftreet.
Llewellin and Son, *Wooller-drapers*, 29, High-ftreet.
Llewellin, James, *Ship in Launch*, Hotwell-road.
Llewellin, Thomas, *Thatch'd Houfe*, Limekiln-lane.
Llewellin, Thomas, *Carpenter*, Ditto
Llewellin and Co. *Maltfters and Brewers*, Upper Maudlin-lane.
Llewellin, Thomas, *Catgut-manufaƈturer*, Lamb-ftreet.
Lewis, William, *Accomptant*, 2, Norfolk-ftreet.
Lewis, D. *Metal Fan-light maker*, Charlotte-ftreet, St. Pauls.
Lewis, Joseph, *Accomptant*, Rofemary-ftreet.
Lewis, William, *Pawnbroker*, Penn-ftreet.
Lewis, Thomas, *Three Cups*, Back.
Lewis, Jenkin, *Goat in Armour*, Quay.
Lewis, Elizabeth, *Paftry-cook*, 13, Clare-ftreet.
Lewis, David, *Merchant and Paper-maker*, Bridge-ftreet.
Lewis, George, *Fruiterer*, All-faints-lane, and 2, High-ftreet.
Lewis, John, *Dealer in Spirits*, Broad-ftreet.
Lewis, Richard, *Lodging-houfe*, 5, Dowry-fquare.
Lewis, William, *Lodging-houfe*, Clifton.
Lewis, Simon, *Shopkeeper*, Hotwell-road.

                                         Lewis,

Lewis, George, *Undertaker*, College-ftreet.
Lewis, William, *Carpenter*, Ditto.
Lewis, William and Son, *Taylors*, Small-ftreet.
Lewis, William, *Hair-dreffer*, Ditto.
Lewis, Lodowick, *Taylor*, Lower Maudlin-lane.
Lewis, Margaret, *Ladies' Boarding-school*, Park.
Lewis, John, *Two Trees*, Wilder-ftreet.
Lewis, Penelope, *Ladies' Boarding-fchool*, Somerfet-ftreet.
Lewis, Robert, *Merchant*, 32, Caftle-green.
Lewis, Sarah, *Painter*, Old-market.
Lewis, Mary, *Collar-maker*, Weft-ftreet.
Lewis, William, *Toy-maker*, Baldwin-ftreet.
Lewis, James, *Shoemaker*, Back ftreet.
Lewis, John, *Collar-maker*, Thomas-ftreet.
Lewis, James, *Smith*, Ditto.
Lewis, Elizabeth, *Royal Oak*, Redcliff-ftreet.
Lewis, Evan, *Mason*, Montague-ftreet.
Lewis, Thomas, Gent. Redcliff-hill.
Lewis, William, *Grocer*, Broad-mead.
Lewis, Capt. William, Baldwin-ftreet.
Lewry, Moe, *Watch-maker*, Redcliff-ftreet.
Lewfly, John, *Merchant*, Brunfwick-fquare.
Lewton, Edward, *Woollen-draper*, 44, High-ftreet.
Libbey, Richard, *Cabinet-maker*, Barrs-ftreet
Liebman and Lazarus, *Silverfmiths*, Temple-ftreet
Lilly, Chriftopher, *Maltfter*, Wilder-ftreet.
Lilly and Wills, *Tobacconifts*, Redcliff-ftreet.
Linch, Jofeph, *Wheat Sheaf*, Chriftmas-ftreet.
Line, Richard, *Baker*, Bedminfter-caufeway.
Linford, Edward, *Watch-maker*, Merchant-ftreet.
Linington, Richard, *Swan*, Cyder-houfe-paffage.
Link, Henry, *Brafs-founder*, Thomas-ftreet.
Lintrin, John, *Taylor*, Bedminfter.
Lifcomb, John, *Crab's-well*, Temple-ftreet.
Little, James, *Baker*, Weft-ftreet.
Livett, Andrew and Co. *Taylors and Stay-makers*, Dolphin-ftreet.
Lock, John, *Shoemaker* 73, Caftle-ftreet.
Lockier, M'Aulay, Gee, and Co *Timber-merchants*, Milk-ftr.
Long, Sarah, *Lodging-houfe*, 37, King-ftreet.
Long, Samuel, *Hooper*, Jacob-ftreet.
Long, Ann, *Tyler and Plaifterer*, Thomas-ftreet.
Long, John, *Yeoman*, Renifons-bath.
Longman, George, *Baker*, Temple-ftreet.
Longman, James, *Grocer*, 53, Redcliff-ftreet.
Longrain, Charles, *Pawnbroker*, Ditto.

Lorain,

Lorain, Mary, *Vintner*, Union-ftreet.
Lorymer, James, *Cornfactor*, Redcliff-ftreet.
Lofcombe, Benjamin, Efq. Lower Eafton.
Louden, Samuel, *Accomptant*, Frog-lane.
Lovelace, John, *Hallier*, Bell-avenue.
Lovell, Robert and Co *Pin-manufacturers*, Caftle-green.
Lovell, John, *Ewe and Lamb*, Thomas-lane.
Lovell, Sarah, *Angel Inn*, Redcliff-ftreet.
Lowder, Samuel, Efq. 19, St. Michaels-hill.
Lowdin, Edward, *Accomptant*, Granger's-court, Broad-mead.
Lowther, John, *Baker*, Lawrence-hill.
Lloyd, Enoch, *Taylor*, King-ftreet.
Lloyd, Jofeph, *Bookseller*, 6, Wine-ftreet.
Lloyd, M. *Mimature-painter*, Hotwell-road.
Lloyd, Major William, 6, Montague-ftreet.
Lloyd, Francis, *Taylor*, North-ftreet.
Lloyd, Walter, *Grocer*, Redcliff-ftreet.
Lloyd, William, *Accomptant*, Lodge-ftreet.
Lucas, William, *Hooper*, St. Michaels-hill.
Lucas, William, *Cuftom-houfe officer*, Portland-ftreet
Lucas, Onefephorus, *Dealer in Spirits*, 1, Old-market.
Lucas, Onefephorus, *Leather-seller*, 2, Ditto.
Lucas, Chance, Homer and Coathupe, *Crown and Glafs-bottie-
    manufacturers*, Nicholas-ftreet.
Lucas, Thomas and William, *Hoopers*, Marfh-ftreet.
Lucas, Samuel, *Confectioner*, Bedminfter.
Luce, T. *Mariner*, Pembroke-court.
Luce, Thomas, *White Lion Inn*, Broad-ftreet.
Lucy, John, *Maltfter*, Back-ftreet.
Ludlow, William, *Gent* Montague-ftreet.
Ludlow, Thomas, *Cleik of the Markets*, Cannon-ftreet.
Ludlow, Alice, *Irormonger*, 23, Old-market.
Ludlow, Mr. Edmund, Jacob-ftreet
Lumly, John, *Grocer*, Limekiln-lane.
Lundberry, Magnus, *Broker and Accomptant*, Caftle-green.
Lundberry, Mary, *Lodging-houf.*, 29, Ditto
Lunell, W. P. *Merchant*, Brunfwick-fquare.
Lury, Son, and Hodgetts, *Patten-ring manufactory*, Philadelphia-
    ftreet.
Lury, Elizabeth, *Salt-refiner*, 56, Caftle-ftreet.
Lury, Son, and Hodgetts, *Wholesale Ironmongers, Cutlers and
    Hardwaremen*, Caftle-green.
Lafcombe, Mifs Sarah, 18, Montague-ftreet.
Lee, George, *Bunch of Grapes*, Thomas ftreet.
Lyne, Ferdinand, Gent. Stoney-hill

Lyne,

Lyne, Thomas, *Linen-draper*, 16, Maryport-ftreet.
Lyons, Dominee, *Spanish Interpreter and Limner*, Quay-head
Lyfon, Capt. Philip, 39, Princes-ftreet

M

Maccraken, John, *Grocer*, Narrow Wine-ftreet.
M'Carthy, Charles, *Jeweller and Tea-dealer*, Corn-ftreet.
M'Carthy, Woodhoufe, and Co *Shoemakers*, 23, Clare-ftreet.
M'Carthy, Owen, *Hair-dreffer and Perfumer*, Broad-ftreet
M'Cullom, John, *Merchant*, 42, Queen-fquare.
M'Donough, P. *Ironmonger and Cutler*, 46, Princes-ftreet.
Mackney, John, *Hofe-dealer*, Hotwells.
Macreth, Ann, *Perfumer*, Ditto.
M'Taggart, James, *Merchant*, 14, College-green.
Maddey, John, *Organ-builder*, Cuftom-houfe-avenue
Maddick and Co. *Silk-mercers*, Clare-ftreet.
Maddin, David, *Sugar*, Little Ann ftreet.
Maddocks, John, *Gardener*, Milk-ftreet.
Maddox, John, Efq. Park-row.
Madley, John, *Jolly Sailor*, Guinea-ftreet.
Maflin, Capt. William, 48, Princes-ftreet.
Maggs, Francis, *Shoemaker*, Stokes croft
Maggs, Jofeph, *Lodging-house*, Redland,
Maies, Capt. Charles, Park.
Mairez, Jane, *Lodging-houfe*, 5, Hotwell-parade.
Mais, John, Gent. St. Philips-plain.
Mais, Charles, *Merchant*, 18, Somerfet-fquare
Maifh, Daniel, *Cheefemonger*, 13, Maryport-ftreet.
Maifh, Giles, *Baker*, Lamb-ftreet.
Mallard, John, *Merchant, and Muftard-merchant*, Quay
Mallwood and Perrin, *Haberdafhers*, Hotwell parade
Maltin, Edward, *File-maker*, Cheefe-lane
Manfield, Jofeph, *Boat-builder*, Canrons-marfh.
Manfield, William, *Scotchman's-pack*, St Michae's-hill.
Mann, William, *Mafter of Elbridge's-fchool*, Fort-lane
Mann, James, *Pump and Block-maker*, Redcliff-backs.
Maplefon, Charles, *Cabinet-maker*, Stoney-hill.
Mapowder, Richard, *Star*, Caftle-ftreet.
Marchant, Jacob, *Baker*, North-ftreet.
Margaret, Charles, *Mason*, Lamb-ftreet.
Marklove, J. H. *Trunk and Box-maker*, Small-ftreet.
Marklove, Robert, *Gardener*, Southwell-ftreet.
Marks, Robert, *Tyler and Plafterer*, Rofemary-ftreet.

Marfhall

Marshall, Capt. William, 4, Wells's-street.
Marshall, William, *Mariner*, 1, Oxford-street.
Marshall, Henry, *Excise-officer*, Dove-street.
Marshall, George, *Hair-dresser*, Nicholas-street.
Martin and Jenkins, *Linen-drapers*, Wine-street.
Martin, Hannah, *Tea-dealer*, 13, Peter-street.
Martin, Samuel, *Grocer*, 24, Castle-street.
Martin, Sarah, *Butcher*, Steep-street.
Martin, Edward, Gent. 17, Somerset-street.
Martin, William, *Carpenter*, Lewins-mead.
Martin, John, *Gingerbread-baker*, Great Ann-street.
Martin, Betty, *Ship and Castle*, Earls-mead.
Martin, Capt. Robert, Trenchard-lane.
Masey, William, *Peruke-maker*, 3, Redcliff-hill.
Masey, Philip and Co *Hoopers*, Thomas-street.
Mason, Thomas, *Bell*, Lamb-street
Masters, James, *Accomptant*, West-street.
Masters, Richard, *Accomptant*, College-street.
Masters, James, *Cabinet-maker*, 2, Castle-street.
Masters, John, Gent Bedminster.
Matchin, William, *Potter*, Wilder-street.
Matchin, William, *Clerk of St. James's-church*, Ditto.
Matchin, William, *Callenderer and Glazer*, Elbroad-street.
Matthews, Henry, *Fruiterer*, 4, Broad-street.
Matthews, Edmund, *Butcher*, 20, Christmas-street.
Matthews, Isaac, *Collar-maker*, West-street.
Matthews, George, *Taylor*, Back-street.
Matthews, Robert, *Spread Eagle*, St. Philips-plain.
Matthews, Capt. Simon, 3, Guinea-street.
Matthews, William, *Printer, and Editor of the New Bristol Guide
    and Directory*, 10, Broad-mead.
Mattocks, William, *Excise-officer*, Bedminster.
Maxse, John and Co. *Merchants*, Clare-street-hall, Marsh-street.
Maxse, John, Esq. All-saints-passage.
May, George, *Soap-boiler and Chandler*, Hotwell-road,
May, E. and C. *Milliners*, 2, St. Augustines-back
May, and Son, *Carpenters*, Wilder-street.
Maybury, William, *Silk-dyer*, Wine-street.
Maynard, William, Gent. 34, Milk-street.
Maynard, Joseph, *Cabinet-maker*, St. Philips-plain.
Maynard, William, *Potter and Chimney-mould maker*, Bread-street.
Mease, Matthew, *Wine-merchant*, Orchard-street.
Meecham, John, *Scrivener*, Trenchard-lane.
Melsom, Charles, *Auctioneer*, Kingsdown.
Melsom, Edward, *Grocer*, Thomas-street.

H   Mentor,

Mentor, Capt. Edward, Orchard-street.
Merchant, Isaac, *Ship*, Earl-street.
Merchant, Richard, Esq. 13, St. James's-square.
Mercy, Ann, *Milliner*, 9, Broad-street
Meredith, John, *Staffordshire-warehouse*, 33, Quay.
Meredith, Daniel, *Wire-worker*, Glocester-lane.
Meredith, Edward, *Pork-butcher*, Thomas-street.
Meredith, Jacob, *Last-maker*, Maryport-church-yard.
Meredith, Solomon, *Woollen-draper*, Ditto.
Mereweather, Samuel, *Cork-cutter*, King-street, & Redcliff-street
Mereweather, Isaac, *Butcher*, Redcliff-street
Merrick, Thomas, *Hemp and Flax-dresser*, Back.
Merrick, William, *Mayor's-officer*, Marlborough-street.
Merrick, Robert, *Baker*, Lewins-mead.
Merrick, Thomas, *Butcher*, Butcher-row.
Merrick, William, *Carpenter*, Redcliff-hill.
Merrychurch, James, *Shoemaker*, Montague-street.
Metford, William, *Butcher*, Temple-street.
Mettam, John, *Bear and Ragged Staff*, Peter-street.
Meyerhoff, Diederick, *Merchant*, King-street.
Michael and Leonard, *Pork-butchers*, Bridewell-lane.
Miles, Philip John, *Merchant*, Queen-square, and Clifton-hill.
Miles, William, *Merchant*, 　　 Ditto, and Clifton-down.
Miles, Thomas, *Custom-house officer*, 36, Stokes-croft.
Miles, William and Co. *Sugar-refiners*, Lewins-mead.
Miles, Mr. William, St. Michael's-hill.
Millard, William, *Cabinet-maker*, Maryport-street.
Millard, James, *Baker*, Narrow Wine-street.
Millard, Elizabeth, *Butcher*, 33, Redcliff-street
Millard, Thomas, *Currier*, 141, Ditto.
Millard and Co. *Soap and Candle-manufacturers*, 142, Ditto.
Milleman, George, *Accomptant*, 2, Gay-street.
Miller, John, *Confectioner*, Hotwells.
Miller, William, *Mason*, North-street.
Miller, Benjamin, *Anchor*, Great Georges-street.
Miller, John, *Wine-merchant*, Bedminster.
Miller and Sweet, *Nursery and Seedsmen*, Durdham-down
Mills, Thomas, *Bookseller*, Corn-street
Mills, William, *Baker*, College-street
Mills, Fanny, *Ladies' Boarding-school*, Park-street.
Mills, William, jun. *Baker*, St. Augustines-back.
Mills, Elizabeth, *Gardener*, Upper Maudlin-lane.
Mills, William, *Baker*, Broad Ware.
Mills, James, *Baker*, Marsh-street.
Mills, Harry, *Plume of Feathers*, 58, Redcliff-street.

Minor

Minor, William, *Painter*, Tower-ftreet.
Mitchell, William, *Lodging-houfe*, Hotwells.
Mitchell, Francis, *Shoemaker*, Temple-ftreet.
Mitton, John, *Glazier*, St. James's-back.
Moger, Thomas, *Carpenter*, Charlotte-ftreet, St Paul.
Mogg, Abraham, *Lodging-houfe*, Kingfdown-parade.
Mogg, Abraham, *Sugar-loaf*, Nicholas-ftreet.
Monday, John, *Painter*, Wade-ftreet.
Monday, Henry, *Carpenter*, Bedminfter.
Monday, Sarah, *Coffee Pot*, Ditto.
Money, William, Efq. Clifton
Montpelier, Stephen, *Crown*, Lawrence-hill.
Moon, James, *Tanner*, Elbroad-ftreet.
Moore, Jofeph, *Pump-maker*, Queen-ftreet.
Moore, Thomas, *Gardener*, Southwell-ftreet.
Moore, John, *Corn-factor*, 4, Jamaica-ftreet.
Moore, Mary, *Bank Tavern*, John-street.
Moore, William and Co. *Rectifiers*, Lewins-mead.
Moore, John, *Currier*, Christmas-street.
Moore, Caleb, *Accomptant*, Redcrofs-ftreet.
Moore, Jofeph, *Accomptant*, Queen-ftreet
Moore, Thomas, *Tyler and Plaifterer*, Bread-ftreet.
Moore, William, *General Elliott*, Bedminfter.
Morgan, George, *Sugar-boiler*, Milk-ftreet.
Morgan, John, *King's-head*, Rofemary-ftreet.
Morgan, William, *Wine-cooper*, 41, Queen-fquare.
Morgan, John, *Vintner*, Wine-street.
Morgan, John, *Watch-maker*, 31, High-ftreet.
Morgan, Sarah, *Milliner*, 23, Ditto
Morgan, Richard, *Bell Tavern*, Broad-ftreet
Morgan, James, *Wine-merchant*, 43, Princes-ftreet.
Morgan, Thomas, *Adam and Eve*, Hotwel's.
Morgan, Thomas, *Spring Gardens*, Hotwell-road.
Morgan, James, Efq 6, Great Georges-ftreet.
Morgan, George, *Confectioner*, St. Auguftines-back.
Morgan, William, *Cuftom-houfe officer*, Frog-lane.
Morgan, Simon, *Coach-mafter*, Ditto,
Morgan, James, Gent. Horfield-lane.
Morgan and Stephens, *Maltfters*, Upper Maudlin-lane.
Morgan, Philip, *Mason*, Earl-ftreet.
Morgan, James, *Pawnbroker*, St. James's-church-yard.
Morgan, Ann, *Prince Eugean*, Hoft-ftreet.
Morgan, William, *Cabinet-maker*, Narrow Wine-ftreet.
Morgan, John, *Watch-maker*, Broad Ware.
Morgan, Thomas, *White Lion*, St. James's-back.

H 2

Morgan.

Morgan, George, *Maltster*, Jacob-ftreet.
Morgan, Edward, *Landing-waiter*, 8, Guinea-ftreet.
Morgan, William, *Red Cow*, Bedminfter.
Morgan, Elizabeth, *Black Swan*, Baptift-mills.
Morgan, John, *Maltfter*, 18, Berkely-fquare.
Morgan, William, *Pawnbroker*, Broad-mead.
Morley, Elizabeth, *Ship and Bull*, Quay.
Morris, Peter and Son, *Carpenters*, York-ftreet.
Morris, Ann, *Grocer*, Milk-ftreet.
Morris, William, *Taylor*, Penn-ftreet.
Morris,   *Hair-dreffer*, Manfion-houfe-ftreet.
Morris, Thomas, *Linen-draper*, 2, Peter-ftreet.
Morris, Henry, *Mariner*, Griffin-lane.
Morris, William, Gent. Wilder-ftreet.
Morris, John, *Taylor*, Dove-ftreet.
Morris, John, *Curious-cabinet*, Nicholas-ftreet.
Morris, Samuel, *Excife-officer*, Cathay-parade.
Morris, James, *Accomptant*, Ditto.
Morris, Nathaniel, 5, Somerfet-place.
Morrow, Richard, *Cabinet-maker*, Peter-street.
Morrow, Thomas, *Salesman*, 1, Castle-street.
Morfe, James, *Accomptant*, Stoney-hill.
Morfton, Robert, *Accomptant*, Ditto.
Mortimore, Edward, *Accomptant*, Queen-street.
Morton, Daniel, *Butcher*, 2, Christmas-street.
Mofs and Lacy, *Maltfters*, Queen-ftreet.
Mound, William, *Pawnbroker*, Penn-ftreet.
Mountain, Abraham, *Ship-smith*, Brick-street.
Mountjoy, Martha, *Lodging-houfe*, 17, Hillgrove-ftreet.
Mountjoy, John, *Plume of Feathers*, Old-market.
Mounfher, James, *Cuftom-houfe officer*, Tinkers-clofe.
Moxam, Jofeph, Efq. 13, Hillgrove-ftreet.
Moxam, Paul, *Mealman*, Old-market.
Moxham, William and Co. *Rectifiers*, Thomas-street.
Moyes, James, *Mariner*, 9, Beaufort-court.
Mugridge, John, *Hair-manufactory*, Horfe-fair.
Mulford, Richard, *Grocer*, Temple-ftreet.
Mullens and Son, *Goldsmiths*, 21, High-ftreet.
Mullens,   *Dealer in Muffins*, Lucky-lane.
Mullis, William, *Boar's-head*, Limekiln-lane.
Munckley, Samuel, *Merchant*, Queen-fquare.
Murch, Ann, *Bull*, Great Georges-ftreet.
Murphey, Jane, *Cloaths-fhop*, Quay
Murphey, James, *Irifh Provifion-factor and Hallier*, Princes-ftreet.
Murray, James, *Quill-manufacturer*, Temple-backs.

Murray,

Murray, William, *Mariner*, 5, Beaufort-court.
Murphey, James, *Mariner*, Pembroke-court.
Muito, Richard, *Lodging-house*, Clifton.

N

Naish, Ann, *Hosier*, 5, High-street.
Naish, Edmund, *Tanner*, Traitors-bridge.
Nangle, Nathaniel, Gent Marsh-street.
Napper, George, *Linen-draper*, 3, Castle-street.
Napper, William, *Mealman*, West-street.
Nash, Ezekiel, Gent 5, Cumberland-street.
Nash, Simon, *Hooper*, Denmark-street.
Nash, John, Gent Park-hill-house.
Nash, *Hooper*, Redcliff-street.
Nash, Goodwin, *Cabinet-maker*, Lodge-street.
Naylor, Castle, and Co *Distillers*, Cheese-lane.
Neal, John, *Ship*, Small-street.
Neat, John, *Farrier*, Limekiln-lane, and Durdham-down.
Neat, Walter, *Livery Stable-keeper*, Merchant-street.
Nelmes, Richard, Esq. 6, King-square.
Nelson, Capt. John, Trinity-street.
Nevill, Henry, *Taylor and Habit-maker*, St. Augustines-place.
New, Miller, and Co *Wine-merchants*, Redcliff-street.
New, Samuel, *Merchant*, Old-market.
Newall, John, *Cabinet-maker*, Cock and Bottle-lane.
Newall, John, *Merchant*, 11, Somerset-square.
Newall, Richard, *Wine-merchant*, Orchard-street.
Newcomb, John, *Cornfactor*, Lamb-street.
Newell, Sarah, *Ship*, Marsh-street.
Newton, Thomas, *Harp and Crown*, Wade-street.
Newton, Isaac, *Shuttle*, Pennywell-lane.
Niblett, Catharine, *Butcher*, Butcher-row.
Niblett, Daniel, *Butcher*, Lamb-street.
Nicholas, John and Co. *Glass-bottle manufacturers*, Limekiln-lane.
Nicholas, David, *King's-head*, Back-street.
Nichols, Edward, *Butcher*, Redcliff-street.
Nichols, Mary, *Lodging-house*, Horfield-lane.
Nichols, Catharine, *Pastry-cook*, 26, Broad-street.
Nickless, John, *Victualler*, Cyder-house-passage.
Night, John, *Tea-dealer*, Wine-street.
Noble, Sarah, *Stay-maker*, Rosemary-street.
Noble, John, Esq *Alderman*, Limekiln-lane
Noble, Thomas, *Umbrella-maker*, Sims's-alley.
Nock, Mary, *Jolly Nailors*, West-street.

Nonmus,

Nonmus, Abraham, *Grocer*, Princes-street.
Nonmus, Isaac, *Mariner*, 1, Hanover-street.
Norman, John, *Cutler and Hardwareman*, High-street.
Norman, George, *Glass-house*, Thomas-street.
Norman, Isaac, *Ostrich*, Trimm-mills.
Norman, Onesiphorus, *Insurance-broker*, All-saints-passage.
Norris, William, *Butcher*, West-street.
Northcote, Richard, *Maltster*, 7, Redcrofs-street.
Northcote, John, *Hair-dresser*, Black-friers.
Norton, Joseph, *Stay-maker*, Philadelphia-street.
Norton, James, *Bookseller, Stationer, and State Lottery-office*, Wine-
   street.
Norton, William, *Shoemaker*, 21, St. Augustines-back.
Norton, Thomas, *Hair-dresser*, 38, Castle-green.
Norton, William, *Glazier*, New-street.
Norton, Peter, *Silk-dyer*, Broad-mead.
Norton's *Picture and Print-rooms*, Ditto.
Nowell, Charles, Esq. Durdham-down.
Nowlan, Michael, *Attorney*, 17, Princes-street.
Noyes, Robert, *Merchant*, 11, Trinity-street.
Nurs, John, *Swan*, St. James's-back.
Nutt, Thomas, *Butcher*, 14, Castle-street.

O

Oakley, John, *Tobacco-pipe maker*, Lewins-mead.
Ogborn, Samuel, *Cabinet-maker*, 5, Cathay.
Oldfield, William, *Talbot*, Redcliff-hill.
Oldham and Whitaker, *Haberdashers*, 57, Wine-street.
Oliver, Ridout, and Oliver, *Linen-drapers*, 1, High-street.
Oliver, Ridout, and Oliver, *Linen-merchants*, Maryport-street.
Oliver, Thomas, Esq. Park-street.
Oliver, Thomas, Gent. 5, Redcrofs-street.
Onion, Thomas, *Dealer in Spirits*, 8, Bath-street.
Organ, Rachael, *Champion of Wales*, Quay.
Orlidge, Joseph, *Wine-merchant*, Small-street.
Ormerod, Thomas, *Lodging-house*, 2, Hotwell-parade.
Ormerod, Lawrence, *Lodging-house*, 3, Albermarle-row.
Ormond, Roger, Gent. 15, St Michaels-hill.
Ormond, John, Gent. Marlborough-street.
O'Ryan, Thomas, *Merchant*, 7, Trinity-street.
Ofmond, William, *Artificial Florist, and Teacher of Fancy work*,
   St. James's church-yard.
Ofmund, Samuel, *Taylor*, Guinea-street.
Overend, William and Co. *Linen-merchants*, Shannon-court.
                                          Owen,

wen, John, *Taylor*, 21, Broad-ſtreet.
wen, Samuel, *Cabinet-maker*, Caſtle-ditch.
wen, William, *Maltſter*, Cheeſe-lane.
xford, William, Eſq. 6, Beaufort-court.

P

acker, Robert, *Red Lyon*, Lawrence-hill.
acker, Joſeph, *Butcher*, Gloceſter-lane.
adfield, Robert, *Taylor*, Weſt-ſtreet
admore, James, *Glaſs Engraver*, Somerſet-ſquare.
age, John, *Merchant*, 59, Queen-ſquare.
age, Ann, *Milliner*, 19, High-ſtreet.
age, Samuel, *Gun-maker*, Bridewell-lane.
age, John, *Brandy-merchant*, Thomas-ſtreet.
agg, James, *Maſon*, St Michaels-hill.
ainter, William, *Upholder*, Back.
ainter and Huggins, *Upholders*, St Auguſtines-back.
ainter, William, *Merchant*, St. Michaels-hill.
alatine, Highman, *Quill-manufacturer*, Temple-ſtreet.
aley, Richard, *Salt Lee-aſh manufacturer*, St. Philips.
allings, Henry, *Cabinet-maker*, Newgate-ſtreet.
almer, Elizabeth, *Bookſeller*, 15, Wine-ſtreet.
almer, Arthur, *Woollen-draper*, 10, Corn-ſtreet.
almer, James, *Woollen-draper*, 28, Ditto
almer, Robert, Eſq. 8, Kingtons-buildings.
almer, John Jordan, *Accomptant*, Stokes-croft.
almer, William, *Taylor*, John-ſtreet.
almer, Thomas, *Jeweller*, 13, Ditto.
almer, William, *Three Block-birds*, Elbroad-ſtreet.
almer, Arthur, *Dealer in Spirits*, Nicholas-ſtreet,
almer, Edward, *Maltſter*, 92, Redcliff-ſtreet.
almer, James, *Ironmonger*, Ditto
almer, James, *Shop*, Redcliff-hill.
anting, Joſeph, *Taylor*, 42, Montague-ſtreet.
anting, Joſeph, *Carpenter*, 38, Lewins-mead.
apps, George, *Hoſier*, Wine-ſtreet.
arfitt, John, *Brazier*, Quay.
arfitt, Benjamin, *Maſon*, St. James's-ſtreet.
aris, Rachael *Lodging-houſe*, Durdham-down
arker, John, *Farrier*, Barrs-ſtreet
arker, John, *Shoemaker*, Broad-ſtreet.
arker, Mary, *Lodging-houſe*, 9, College-green
arker, William, *Dealer in Spirits*, Thomas-ſtreet.

Parker,

Parker, Robert, *Golden Fleece*, Redcliff-backs.
Parkhouse, Richard, *Butcher*, Chriftmas-ftreet.
Parkhouse, John, *Brazier*, Old-market.
Parr and Wright, *Engravers*, Union-ftreet.
Parry, Betty, *Rofe and Crown*, Merchant-ftreet.
Parry, Tozer, and Co. *Tin-plate-workers*, 26, Corn-ftreet.
Parry, William, Gent. 9, Dighton-ftreet.
Parry, Cole, and Co. *Diftillers*, Temple-ftreet.
Parfley, James, *Peruke-maker*, Broad-ftreet.
Parfons, William, *Linen-drap'n*, Wine-ftreet.
Parfons, John, *Stationer*, Baldwin-ftreet.
Parfons and Hurles, *Linen-merchants*, High-ftreet.
Parfons, William, *Merchant*, 7, College-green.
Parfons, Richard, *Pawnbroker*, Great Ann-ftreet.
Paffey, Mary, *Pawnbroker*, Old-market.
Pater, Henry, jun *Upholder*, Wine-ftreet, and 4, Bath-ftreet.
Patience, Ann, *Crofs Keys*, Temple-ftreet
Patience and Moore, *Haberdafhers*, Weft-ftreet.
Patridge, Charles, Efq. 3, College-green
Patridge, Nathaniel, *Tin-plate-worker*, Broad-ftreet.
Paty, William, *Architect*, Limekiln-lane.
Patty, James, *Carver and Gilder*, Broad-mead.
Payne, Charles, Efq 4, Queens-parade.
Payne, Edward, *Butcher*, Weft-ftreet.
Payne, Henry, *Glass-manufacturer*, St Philips.
Payton, Betty, *Dealer in Spirits*, Bath-ftreet.
Payton, William, *Shoemaker*, 43, Caftle-ftreet.
Peace, Peter, *Brufh-maker*, 83, Ditto.
Peach, Robert, Efq. 9, Barton.
Peake, Robert, *Mariner*, College-ftreet.
Pearce, Capt. Henry, 57, Queen-fquare
Pearce, Thomas, *Lodging-houfe*, 11, King-ftreet
Pearce, Charles and Co *Haberdafhers*, 10, Clare-ftreet.
Pearce, Stephen, *Cuftom-houfe officer*, Eugean-ftreet.
Pearce, Earl, *Potter*, Bread-ftreet.
Pearce, Benjamin, *White Hart*, Bedminfter-caufeway.
Pearce, Jofeph, *Accomptant*, Greville-ftreet.
Pearl, Francis, *Carpenter*, Redcliff-hill.
Pearfe, John, *Mafon*, Charlotte-ftreet.
Pearfon, Holbech, and Co. *Coventry-warehoufe*, Broad-ftreet.
Peel, Edward, *Linen-draper*, Wine-ftreet.
Pember, William, *Sugar-refiner*, Brunfwick-fquare, Counter in
    Wilder-ftreet.
Pendry, Thomas, *Salt-refiner*, Thomas-ftreet.
Pendry, Thomas, *Excife-officer*, 6, Somerfet-place.

Penington,

Penington, **William,** *Master of the Ceremonies,* Dowry-square.
Penington, Isaac, *Baker,* Hotwell-road.
Penny, Charles, *Watch-maker,* Broad-ftreet.
Penny, **William,** *Mason,* Hotwell-road.
Penton, David, *Taylor,* Caftle-ditch.
Pepleton, William, *Tripe-merchant,* New-ftreet.
Percivall, John, *Glafs-cutter,* Union-ftreet.
Percivall, John, *Mufician,* Pipe-lane.
Perinton, John, *White Lion Inn,* Thomas-ftreet.
Perkins, Capt. Jofeph, 17, Trinity-ftreet.
Perkins, Thomas, *Merchant,* Oxford-ftreet.
Perks, Thomas, *Butcher,* Bridewell-lane.
Perratt, George, *Baker,* Lower Maudlin-lane.
Perrett, William, *Taylor,* Philadelphia-ftreet.
Perrin, William, *Three Kings,* Quay-head
Perrin, Bence, and Co. *Curriers,* Broad-mead.
Perrins, John, *Ship,* Redcliff-hill.
Perry, William, *Hat-manufacturer,* 23, Caftle-ftreet.
Perry, Robert, *Hair-dreffer,* 64, Ditto.
Perry, William, *Currier,* 69, Ditto.
Perry, James, *Hooper,* 18, Maryport-ftreet.
Perry, Thomas, *Drawing-mafter,* Park-ftreet.
Perry, Leonard, *Coach-mafter,* Quakers-friers.
Peters, William, *Tin-plate worker,* Thomas-ftreet.
Peters, Edward, *Baker,*   Ditto.
Peters, John, *Caftom-houfe officer,* 4, Redcliff-hill.
Peters and Pook, *Undertakers,*   Ditto.
Petherick, John, *Lodging-houfe,* 9, Denmark-ftreet.
Pewters, Jofeph, *Shoemaker,* 1, Jamaica-ftreet.
Phillemore, Ifaac, *Hofier,* Redcliff-ftreet.
Phillips, Jacob, *Windmill,* Bedminfter.
Phillips, William, *Block and Pump-maker,* Quay.
Phillips, Jacob, *Shoemaker,* Ditto.
Phillips, Robert, *Wheelwright,* Broad-mead,
Phillips, Catharine, *Angel,* High-ftreet.
Phillips and Grift, *Brokers and Accomptants,* Broad-ftreet.
Phillips, Thomas, *Accomptant,* St. Auguftines-place.
Phillips and Stuckey, *Salt-merchants,* Quay-head.
Phillips, William, Gent. Upper Maudlin-lane.
Phillips, William, *Mason,* Kingfdown.
Phillips, Edward, *Bright-fmith,* Lawrence-hill.
Phillips, William, *Cheefe-factor,* Baldwin-ftreet.
Phippen, Robert, *Wool-ftapler,* Bedminfter.
Phipps, James, *Crown,* Thomas-ftreet
Pidding and Son, *Carpenters,* Glocefter-lane.

I

Piercy,

Piercy, Lieut. Richard, *Royal Navy*, 14, Paul-ftreet.
Pigienit, Mrs. Catharine, 4. Granby-place, Hotwells.
Pike, Jofiah, *Cuftom-houfe officer*, Hoft-ftreet.
Pike, James, *Tyler and Plaifterer*, Old-market.
Pimm, James, *Broker*, Pithay.
Pinchin, James, *Ship*, Newmarket-paffage.
Pine, William, *Printer of the Briftol Gazette*, Narrow Wine-ftreet
Pine, Mr. William, 3, King-fquare.
Pink, William, *Bright-fmith*, Caftle-ditch.
Pinnell, John, *Hooper*, Little King-ftreet.
Pinnock, John, *Perfumer*, 2, St. James's-parade.
Piper, William, *Grocer*, 39, Old-market.
Pippet, Richard, *Baker*, Temple-ftreet.
Pittman, Mr. James, 3, Southwell-ftreet.
Plaifter, Richard, Gent. Redcliff-parade.
Player, John, *Dealer in Spirits*, Caftle-ftreet.
Player, Edward, *Porter-merchant*, King-ftreet.
Plumley, Edward, *Furrier*, 8, High-ftreet.
Plumley, George, *Dealer in Spirits*, Redcliff-ftreet
Plummer, William, *Grocer*, 20, Hillgrove-ftreet.
Pobjoy, Robert, *Mason*, Marfh-ftreet.
Pocock, Capt. William, 6, College-ftreet.
Point, John, *Cabinet-maker*, Stokes-croft.
Pointing, Thomas, *Stay-maker*, Philadelphia-ftreet,
Pollard, William and Co. *Sail-makers*, Quay.
Pollard, William, *Ship-broker*, Ditto.
Pollard, Samuel, *Linen-draper*, Barton.
Pomroy, George, *Livery Stable-keeper*, Pithay.
Poole, Nicholas, *Haberdafher*, 20, Broad-ftreet.
Poole, William, *Carpenter*, Denmark-ftreet.
Poole, Thomas, Gent. Black-friers.
Poole, William, *Bright-fmith*, Barton-alley.
Poole, Mary, *Coach and Horfes*, Broad-mead.
Pope, Thomas, *Carpenter*, Penn-ftreet.
Pope, William, *Hair-dreffer and Perfumer*, St. Auguftines-place
Pope, Thomas, *Carpenter*, Marlborough-ftreet,
Pope, Philip, *Accomptant*, Dove-ftreet.
Pope, Andrew, Gent. 6, St. James's-fquare.
Pope, Jofeph, *Popes-head and Pelican Inn*, Thomas-ftreet.
Portch and Co. *Fringe-manufacturers*, Peter-ftreet.
Porter, George, *Salesman*, Quay.
Porter, Benjamin, *Painter*, St. Michaels-hill.
Porter, John, *Three Kings Inn*, Thomas-ftreet.
Porter, John, *Corn factor*, Bedminfter.
Potter, Richard, *Pawnbroker*, Redcliff-hill.

Potts, Lawrence, *Cutler*, Quay.
Pounsberry, James, *Baker*, Temple-street.
Pounsberry, Samuel, *Mealman*, Tower-street.
Pounsett, William, *Mayor's-officer*, Glocester-street.
Powell, T. *Tyler and Plaisterer*, Milk-street.
Powell, Jane, *Full Moon*, Broad-street.
Powell, Mr. Samuel, Hotwells.
Powell, John, *Lodgings*, 7 and 8, Princes-place, Clifton.
Powell, Joseph, *Lodgings*, 4 and 5, Sion-hill.
Powell, John, *Lodging-house*, Clifton.
Powell, john, *Glazier*, Hotwell-road.
Powell, John, Esq. *Collector of the Customs*, College-green.
Powell, Joseph, *Bright-smith*, Denmark-street.
Powell, Martha, *Midwife*, Culver-street.
Powell, Edward, *Bear*, Earl-street.
Powell, Timothy, Gent. Redcliff-hill.
Powell, John, *Bird in the Hand*, Ditto.
Powell, Joshua and Co. *Wine-merchants*, Redcliff-street.
Powell, Boon, *Cork-cutter*, Ditto.
Powell, Thomas, *Whitesmith*, Ditto.
Power, Edward, *Mariner*, Back.
Power, Elizabeth, *Staffordshire-warehouse*, Ditto.
Power, James, *Hosier*, 12, St. Augustines-back.
Pownall, William, *Accomptant*, 6, Carolina-row.
Pratten, Mark, *Shoemaker*, Lawrence-hill.
Preece, John, *Common-brewer*, King-street.
Price, Adam, Gent. 4, Cumberland-street.
Price, Thomas, *Taylor*, 2, Newfoundland-street.
Price and Morgan, *Hosiers and Glovers*, Clare-street.
Price, William, *Brightsmith*, Host-street.
Price, Thomas, *New Globe*, Christmas-street.
Price, Timothy, *Hooper*, Lawrence-hill.
Price, Elizabeth, *Ironmonger*, Thomas-street.
Price, Charles, *Fourteen Stars*, Counter-slip.
Prichard, Edmund, *Accomptant*, Milk-street.
Prichard, E. and T. *Staffordshire-warehouse*, Quay.
Prichard, Edmund, *Deal-merchant*, 43, College-green.
Prichard, Thomas, *Brush-maker*, Nicholas-street.
Prideaux, Thorn, and Co. *Silk-mercers*, Wine-street.
Prideaux, John, *Merchant*, Horfield-lane.
Prideaux, Francis, Gent. 44, Montague-street.
Priddey and Adamson, *Salt-merchants and Wharfingers*, Small-str.
Priddey, Robert, *Baker*, Old-market,
Priest, Martin, *Watch-maker*, St. Michaels-hill.
Priest, William, *Watch-maker*, Bridewell-lane.

Prince,

Prince, Samuel, Gent. 21, St. Michaels-hill.
Prince, Sarah, *Lodging-house*, Montague-ftreet.
Prifk, Thomas, *Shoemaker*, 37, Maryport-ftreet.
Pritchard, William, *Ironmonger*, Quay-ftreet.
Pritchard, Samuel, *Lamb and Flag*, Frog-lane.
Pritchard, William, *King David*, St. Michaels-hill.
Pritchard, Samuel, *Grocer*, Marlborough-street.
Pritchard, Sufannah, *Poulterer*, 2, St. James's church-yard.
Pritchard, William, *Grocer*, 3, Ditto.
Pritchard, John, *Hallier*, Traitors-bridge.
Privett, Edith, *Midwife*, Philadelphia-ftreet.
Proberts, jamefon, and Co. *Linen-merchants*, Caftle-ftreet.
Proffer, Roger, *Rofe and Crown*, Redcrofs-ftreet.
Proffer, Charles, *Silk-mercer*, 6, Broad-ftreet, & Somerfet-ftreet.
Proffer, Capt. William, 7, Princes-ftreet.
Protheroe, John, *Iron-merchant*, Quay, and Princes-ftreet
Protheroe, Philip, *Merchant*, Great Georges-ftreet.
Protheroe and Claxton, *Weft India-merchants*, Ditto.
Protheroe, Thomas, *Cooper*, St. Auguftines-back.
Prowlin, James, *Coach and Horfes*, Old-market.
Pruft, Capt. Stephen, 8, Trinity-ftreet.
Pugh, Samuel, *Brandy-merchant*, Avon-ftreet.
Pullin, James, *Accomptant*, 5, Trenchard-lane.
Punker, Richard, *White Hart*, Upper Maudlin-lane.
Punter, James, *Tin-plate worker*, Maryport-ftreet.
Purnell, Jane, *Roap-maker*, Back.
Purnell, Matthew, *Night-conftable*, under the Bank.
Purnell, John, *Infurance-broker*, Exchange.

Q

Quarman, Jofeph, *Turner*, Lewins-mead.
Quinton, Michael, *Taylor*, Lodge-ftreet.

R

Radford, William, *Swan*, New-ftreet.
Radmore, Nathaniel, *Port-guager*, Wilder-ftreet.
Rallins, William, *Diftiller*, Upper Maudlin-lane.
Randolph, Mrs. Elizabeth, Redcliff-parade.
Ransford and Sons, *Hat-manufacturers*, Wine-ftreet.
Ransford, Mr. Thomas, 8, Orchard-ftreet.
Ranton, E. and M. *Tea-dealers*, 25, St Auguftines-back.
Rawlings, Thomas, *Carpenter*, Old-market.

Rawlings.

Rawlings, John, *Grocer*, Temple-ftreet.
Rawlins, Edward and Co. *Diftillers*, Redcliff-ftreet.
Rawlins, Richard, *Ship-chandler*, Wapping.
Read, Jofeph, *Accomptant*, Barrs-ftreet.
Read, Jofeph, *Broker*, St James's-back.
Read, Thomas, *Bell*, Broad Ware.
Reading, Thomas, *Taylor*, Hotwells.
Reading, John, *Taylor*, Ditto.
Redford and Bence, *Wholefale Linen-drapers*, 38, Bridge-ftreet.
Reece, Mary, *Lodging-houfe*, Hotwells.
Reed, Elizabeth, *Hair-dreffer*, Princes-ftreet.
Reed, William, *Jeweller*, 28, Clare-ftreet.
Reed, William, Gent. St. Vincents-parade.
Reed, Capt Thomas, 9, Jamaica-ftreet.
Reed, Chiverton, *Butcher*, Bridewell-lane.
Reed, Benjamin, *Watch-maker*, Lawrence-hill.
Reed, William, *Butcher*, Broad-mead.
Rees, John, *Carpenter*, 63, Stokes-croft.
Rees, John, *Excife-officer*, St. Michaels-hill.
Rees, Owen, *Bookfeller, Binder and Stationer*, Wine-ftreet.
Reeve, John, *Collar-maker*, Bedminfter.
Reid, William, *Broker*, All-faints-paffage.
Reily, John and Co. *Sugar-refiners*, Great Georges-ftreet.
Rennifon, Thomas, *Old England Tavern*, Rennifons-bath.
Rex, Jofeph, *London Waggon*, Bedminfter.
Reynolds, Thomas, *Wine-merchant*, Barton.
Reynolds, Frederick, *Lodging-houfe*, Hotwells.
Reynolds, Capt. Thomas, Limekiln-lane.
Rice, Ann, *Stay-maker*, Lower Maudlin-lane.
Rice, John, *Taylor*, Hillgrove-ftreet.
Rice, Francis, *Patten-maker*, Newgate-ftreet.
Rich, John, *Currier*, Broad-mead.
Rich, Robert, *Maltfter*, Barton-ftreet.
Rich, John, *Hofier*, 14, Maryport-ftreet.
Rich, Samuel, *Cornfactor*, 32, Ditto.
Richards, Ann, *Brightsmith*, Philadelphia-ftreet.
Richards, Thomas, *Queen's-head*, Ditto.
Richards, Thomas, *Tobacconift*, 37, Caftle-ftreet.
Richards, William, *Taylor*, Princes-ftreet.
Richards, James, *Grocer*, Hotwells.
Richards, Capt John, 10, College-ftreet.
Richards, Jofeph, *Carpenter*, Montague-ftreet.
Richards, William, *Carpenter*, Earl-ftreet.
Richards, Benjamin, *Grocer*, Horfe-fair.
Richards, Sarah, *Confectioner*, Lawrence-hill.

Richards,

Richards, John, *Brightsmith*, Wade-street,
Richards, Samuel, *Tobacco-pipe maker*, Thomas-street.
Richardson, *Dealer in Spirits*, Broad-street.
Richardson, Maria, *Haberdasher*, 40, Maryport-street.
Richfield, Thomas, *Globe Cellar*, Nicholas-street.
Richmond, William, *Collector of the Salt duties*, St. Augustines place.
Rickards, Jeremiah, *Brightsmith*, Castle-street.
Ricketts and Load, *Tobacconists*, Dolphin-street.
Ricketts, Ewer, and Deering, *Hat-manufacturers*, Clare-street.
Ricketts, Henry, *Plumber*, Lewins-mead.
Ricketts, Richard, Gent. Ashley-court.
Ricketts, Jacob, *Tobacconist*, Old-market.
Riddle, Jacob, *White Hart Inn*, Ditto.
Riddle, William, *Bacon-merchant*, Ashley-court.
Rider, William, *Shoemaker*, West-street.
Ridout, Nicodemus, *Maltster*, Milk-street,
Rigge, Mrs. P. Trinity-street.
Righton, Thomas, *Cabinet-maker*, St Michaels church-yard.
Ring and Carter, *Only manufacturers of Queen's-ware*, Temple-backs.
Ring, Robert, *Hooper*, Thomas-street.
Roach, Thomas, *Accomptant*, Milk-street.
Roach, Isaac, *Shoemaker*, Barrs-street.
Roach, Solomon, *Dock-master*, Hotwell-road.
Roach, George, *Merchant*, Queens-parade.
Roach, John and Son, *Timber-merchants*, St. Augustines-place.
Roach, Abraham, *Dolphin*, Tucker-street.
Roach, John, *Butcher*, St. James's-back.
Roach, George, *Leather-dresser*, Traitors-bridge.
Robe, Sarah, *Perfumer*, 10, Broad-street.
Robe, Archibald, Gent. St. Michaels-hill.
Roberts and Ricketts, *Linen-drapers*, 27, High-street, and 29, Bridge-street.
Roberts, William, Gent. Clifton-hill.
Roberts, David, *Accomptant*, Cannons-marsh.
Roberts, William, *Brewer*, Horfield-lane.
Roberts, Thomas, *Wine-merchant*, 3, Stokes-croft.
Roberts, Hugh, *Ship*, Wade-street.
Roberts, John, *Gardener*, St. Philips.
Roberts, John, *Hair-dresser*, Redcliff-street.
Roberts, Capt. James, Trenchard-lane.
Roberts, Thomas, *Cabinet-maker*, Merchant-street.
Robertson, Samuel, *Sail-maker*, 40, St. Michaels-hill.
Robertson, Capt. William, Terill-street.

Robins,

Robins, Charles, *Cabinet-maker*, 25, Milk-ftreet.
Robins, John, *Lodging-houfe*, 1, Hotwell-crefcent.
Robins, Thomas, *Maltfter*, Lewins-mead.
Robinfon, John, *Fifhmonger*, Quay.
Robinfon, Richard, *Ship-joiner*, Ditto.
Robinfon, Mary, *Grocer*, Maryport-ftreet.
Rodway, Joyce, *Haberdafher*, Redcliff-hill.
Roe, Robert, *Cornifh Mount*, Quay.
Rogers, Thomas, *Dock Gates*, Hotwell-road.
Rogers, James, *Merchant*, College-green.
Rogers, Capt. Richard, Culver-ftreet.
Rogers, George, *Three Tuns*, Lewins-mead.
Rogers, John, *Cheefe-factor*, Back-hall, and Redcliff-ftreet.
Rogers, Sarah, *Star*, St. James's-back.
Rogers, Jacob and Son, *Vinegar-makers*, Traitors-bridge.
Rogers, Samuel and Co. *Brewers*, Temple-backs.
Rogers, Capt. Richard, *Crow*, Crow-lane.
Rolls, Samuel, Gent. Cathay.
Ronaldfon, Capt. Thomas, Limekiln-lane.
Rooks, Samuel, *Linen-draper*, Wine-ftreet.
Room, William, *Clerk of the Parifh*, Bedminfter.
Room, James, *Accomptant*, Orchard-ftreet.
Room, Mr. Walter, 6, Chapel-row, Hotwells.
Ropton, Thomas, *King's-arms*, Thomas-ftreet.
Rofe, John, *Printer*, Broad-mead.
Rofe, William, *Plumber*, Merchant-ftreet.
Rofe, Sufannah, *Bunch of Grapes*, Bedminfter.
Rofemond, Philip, *French Academy*, Marlborough-ftreet.
Rofler, Charles, *Shoemaker*, 11, Broad-mead.
Rofliter, John, *Little Tower*, Quay.
Rotely, Lewis, *Oftrich Tavern*, Durdham-down.
Rothley, Thomas, Efq. Lower-green.
Routh, George, *Printer*, Shannon-court.
Routh, William, *Printer of Sarah Farley's Journal*, Bridge-ftreet.
Routh, William, *Grocer*, Hotwell-road.
Routh, S. *Grocer*, St. Auguftines-back
Routh, James, *Cabinet-maker*, Chriftmas-ftreet.
Rowe, George, *Gardener*, Newfoundland-ftreet.
Rowe, Mary, *Duke of Cornwall*, Quay.
Rowland, Richard, *Mathematical Inftrument-maker*, Ditto.
Rowland, Mary, *Dealer in Spirits*, Ditto.
Rowland, William, *Carpenter*, Kingtons-buildings
Rowland, Robert, *Dealer in Spirits*, Redcliff-ftreet.
Rudhall, Ann, *Tea and China-warehoufe*, Briftol-bridge.
Rudhall, John, *Printer of Felix Farley's Journal*, Small-ftreet.

Rudhall,

Rudhall, Anthony, *Baker*, Bedminfter.
Rugg, Thomas, *Hair-dreffer*, Thomas-ftreet.
Runwa, Capt. Benjamin, Stokes-croft.
Ruffell, James, *Merchant*, Unity-ftreet.
Ruffell, Capt. John, 10, Wells's-ftreet.
Ruffell, John, Gent. Dove-ftreet.
Ruffell, John, *Pawnbroker*, Lewins-mead.
Ruffell, Thomas, *Crofs Keys*, Lawrence-hill.
Rutter, Thomas, *Bellows and Brufh-maker*, Caftle-ftreet.
Ryland, John, *Linen-draper*, Dove-ftreet.

S

Sadler, John, *Repofitory for Horfes, &c.* College-ftreet.
Safford. I. T. *Dentift*, Queen-fquare.
Sainfbury, Samuel, *Baker*, Unity-ftreet, St. Philips.
Saint, Thomas, *Cotton-manufacturer*, Little Georges-ftreet.
Sale, Capt. George, College-ftreet.
Salmon, Thomas, *Currier*, 44, Old-market.
Salmon, Robert, Gent. 11, Queen-fquare.
Salworth, George, *Hair-dreffer*, Broad-ftreet.
Samuel, Benjamin, *Furrier*, 3, Bath-ftreet
Samuel, Jacob, *Glass Engraver*, Temple-ftreet.
Sandall, Arthur, *Corn-chandler*, Weft-ftreet.
Sandell, Thomas, Gent. Elbroad-ftreet.
Sanders, James and Co. *Floor-cloth manufacturers*, Bath-ftreet
Sanders, William, Gent. Bedminfter.
Sandys, Samuel, *Lace and Fringe-manufacturer*, Bridge-ftreet
Sangar, John, *Haberdafher*, Nicholas-ftreet.
Sarney, Anthony, *Farrier*, Weft-ftreet.
Sartain, Jofeph, *Baker*, Horfe-fair.
Saunders and Co. *Ironmongers*, Milk-ftreet.
Saunders, Jofeph, *Watch-maker*, Quay.
Saunders, James and Son, *Grocers*, Lamb-ftreet.
Saunders, Thomas and Son, *Seed, Corn, and Hop-merchant,* Bridge-parade.
Savage, Mr. Edward, 4, Pipe-lane.
Savery, John, *Banker*, Orchard-ftreet.
Sayce, Thomas, *Carpenter*, Charles's-ftreet.
Sayer, Francis, *Accomptant*, 25, Caftle-green.
Sayer, Samuel, *Accomptant*, 4, Redcrofs-ftreet.
Sayer, Robert and Co. *Millers*, Trimm-mills.
Schimmelpenning and Co. *Infurance-brokers*, Exchange.
Schimmelpenning, Lambert, Gent. Orchard-ftreet.

Scott

Scott, John, *Accomptant*, James's-ftreet.
Scott, Ifaac, *Carpenter*, Great-gardens.
Scudamore, Rowles, *Barrifter at Law*, 4, Stokes-croft.
Searle, James, *Three Horfe-fhoes*, Rope-walk.
Seaton, William, Gent. Trinity-ftreet.
Seede, Richard, *Organ-builder, and Piano-forte maker*, College-ftreet.
Seede, John, Gent. Beaufort-court.
Selden, Henry, *Turner*, Stokes-croft.
Seley, Charles, *Excife-officer*, St Philips.
Selfe, Elizabeth, *Grocer*, 42, Old-market.
Sellick, Samuel, *Bookfeller*, St. James's-back.
Sellick, Jofiah, *Accomptant*, Hotwell-road.
Sennington, Jofeph, *Tyler and Plaifterer*, World's-end, Clifton.
Sergeant, William, *Collar-maker*, Bedminfter.
Sergeant, Thomas, *Cold-harbour Farm*, Redland.
Sevier, James, *Horse-hair manufacturer*, Caftle-ftreet.
Seward, Frederick, *Painter*, Old King-ftreet.
Seward, Samuel, *City Trumpeter*, Avon-ftreet.
Sewell, James, *Talbot Tavern*, Redcliff-ftreet.
Sewell, Elizabeth, *Chequers*, Redcliff-backs.
Sewell, William, *Boarding-fchool*, Cathay.
Shapland, Jofeph, Gent. Park-ftreet.
Shapland, Chriftopher, *Accomptant*, Montague-ftreet.
Shapland, Harding, and Co. *Soap and Candle-manufacturers*, Old-market.
Shapland, Harding, and Co. *Salt lee-afh manufacturers*, St. Philips
Shapland, Underwood, and Riddle, *Lead-merchants*, Ditto.
Shapland, Harding, and Co's *Soap-manufactory*, Broad-mead
Sharman, John, *Baker*, College-ftreet.
Sharman, Thomas, *Butcher*, Lawrence-hill.
Sharp, William, *Hair-dreffer*, Limekiln-lane.
Sharp, Benjamin, *Baker*, Hoft-ftreet.
Shaw and Son, *Sadlers*, 17, Broad-ftreet.
Shaw, Mary, *Grocer*, Hillgrove-ftreet.
Shaw, Capt. Richard, 7, Pipe-lane.
Shedden, Samuel, *Accomptant*, 34, Stokes-croft.
Shelden John, *Accomptant*, St Philips-plain.
Sheppard, Jofeph, *Stocking-manufacturer*, Corn-ftreet.
Sheppard, J. F. *Milliner*, 2, Broad-ftreet.
Sheppard, George, *Pork-butcher*, 26, Caftle-ftreet.
Sheppard, Jofeph, *Carpenter*, Bridewell-lane.
Sheppard, Mary, *Haberdafher*, Ditto.
Sheppard, John, *Gingerbread-baker*, Lamb-ftreet.
Sheppard, George, *Wheelwright*, Cheefe-lane.

Sherriff,

Sherriff, Edmund. *Writing-master*, Milk-ſtreet.
Sherry. Capt. William, 40, Princes-ſtreet.
Shiercliff, Edward, *Circulating Library*, St. Auguſtines-back
Shill, Henry, *Roſe and Crown*, Bedminſter.
Shilſton, Simon, *Ship*, James's ſtreet.
Shipway, John, *Tea-dealer*, 11, Union-ſtreet
Shorland, Thomas, *Ship*, Pipe-lane.
Shorland, William, *Engineer*, St Philips-place
Short, Elizabeth, *Greyhound*, Cheeſe-lane.
Short, Thomas, *Hat-maker*, Lewins-mead.
Shroll, William, *Sheriff's-officer*, Bedminſter.
Sier, Rachael, *Jolly Tanner*, Great Georges-ſtreet.
Silkſton, Charles, *Livery Stable-keeper*, Hotwell-road.
Simmons, Ann, *Drawing-miſtreſs*, Cumberland-ſtreet
Simmons, Joſeph, *Accomptant*, Unity-ſtreet, St. Philips.
Simpſon, Jonathan, Gent. College-ſtreet
Sims, Capt. John, Butts.
Sims, Thomas, *Merchant*, 10, St. Michaels-hill.
Sims, James, *Carpenter*, Caſtle-green.
Sims, George, *Cabinet-maker*, Thomas-ſtreet.
Sinnot,   *Old Globe*, Chriſtmas-ſtreet
Sircom, William, *Looking-glaſs maker*, Old-market
Sixſmith, Adam, *Lodging-houſe*, Clifton-hill.
Skeel, John, *Shoemaker*, Hotwell-road
Skidmore, Richard, *Maltſter*, Cheeſe-lane.
Skillin, Samuel, *Confectioner*, Broad-ſtreet
Skinner, William, *Basker*, Stephen-ſtreet.
Skinner, Thomas, *Chair-maker*, Tower-ſtreet.
Slade, William, *Whip-maker*, Barrs-ſtreet
Slade, Thomas, *Grocer*, Hotwell-road.
Slade, Henry, *Collar-maker*, Weſt-ſtreet.
Slade, Chriſtopher, *Sadler and Collar-maker*, Bath-ſtreet.
Slayne, William, *Baker*, Old King-ſtreet.
Sleep, Henry, *Baker*, Hotwell-road.
Slocombe, William, *Tin-plate worker*, Bridewell-lane
Slocombe, Capt. Richard, College-ſtreet
Slocombe, William, *Golden Lyra*, 100, Redcliff-ſtreet.
Slocombe, William, *Linen-draper*, Bridge-parade.
Sloper, Richard, *Hat-manufacturer*, Redcliff-ſtreet.
Sloper, William, *Hope Inn*, Redcliff-hill.
Sloper, Richard, *Taylor*, Temple-ſtreet.
Sloper, John, *Glazier*, Ditto.
Sloper, Charles, *Mariner*, Culver-ſtreet.
Slowley, Matthew, *Maltſter*, Lawrence-hill.
Small, Samuel, *Hair-dreſſer*, Lower Maudlin-lane

Smart

mart, Thomas, *Bookseller*, John-ftreet.
mart, Edward, *Glafs-houfe*, Cheefe-lane.
martfoot, Thomas, *Joiner*, Baldwin-ftreet.
martfoot, Thomas, Gent. 3, Oxford-ftreet.
mith, Chriftian, *Butcher*, Old King-ftreet.
mith, George, *Accomptant*, Philadelphia-ftreet.
mith, Catharine, *Lodging-houfe*, 22, Queen-fquare
mith, William, *Prince of Wales*, Back.
mith, Hannah, *Plume of Feathers*, Wine-ftreet.
mith, Parfons, and Smith, *Wholesale Linen-drapers*, High-ftreet.
mith, George, *Haberdafher*, 32, Caftle-ftreet.
mith, Thomas, *Tin-plate worker*, 52, Ditto.
mith, William, *Tin-plate worker*, 59, Ditto.
mith, Timothy, *Stocking-manufacturer*, Ditto.
mith, *Lodging-houfe*, 3, Dowry-fquare.
mith, Ifaac, *Poulterer*, Hotwells.
mith, John, Gent Hotwell-road.
mith, Freeman, Efq. *Sword-bearer*, College-green.
Smith, Cornelius, *Mariner*, Orchard-ftreet.
Smith, Edward, *Mariner*, 12, Park.
Smith, *Grocer*, 9, Chriftmas-ftreet.
Smith, William, *Cock and Bottle*, Caftle-green.
Smith, Martha, *Ironmonger*, Old-market.
Smith, William, *Grocer*, 35, Ditto
Smith, Robert, *Maltfter*, Lawrence-hill
Smith, William, *Grocer*, Nicholas-ftreet
Smith, Robert, *Cheefe-factor*, Ditto.
Smith, John, *Brewer*, Baldwin-ftreet.
Smith, Richard, *Buckle-maker*, Back-ftreet.
Smith, Henry, *Wool-pack*, Eugean-ftreet.
Smith, Jofeph, *Sheriff's-officer*, St, Philips-place.
Smith, Jofeph, *Glass Engraver*, Cathay.
Smith, Ann, *White-horfe*, Bedminfter.
Smyth, Charles, *Cabinet-maker*, Quakers-friers.
Smith, James, *Infurance-broker*, Exchange.
Snelgrove, William, *Wheat Sheaf*, Callowhill-ftreet.
Snelgrove, Ifrael, *Shoemaker*, Hillgrove-ftreet.
Snell, William, *Excife-officer*, Elbroad-ftreet.
Snelling, William, *Trout Tavern*, North-ftreet.
Snigg, James, *Peruke-maker*, Broad-mead.
Snook, J and W. *Wine-merchants*, 28, Broad-ftreet.
Solomon, S. *Linen-draper*, Caftle-ftreet.
Solomon, M. and P. *Lace-dealers*, St. Auguftines-back.
Solomon, Sufannah, *Broker*, Thomas-ftreet
Somerland, Thomas, *Accomptant*, St. Philips-place.

Somers,

Somers, William, *Blue Bowl*, Temple-ftreet.
Somerton, Jofeph, *Printer*, St. Michaels-fteps.
South, William, *Excife-officer*, Park.
Southey, William, *Dealer in Spirits*, College-ftreet.
Sowerby, Samuel, *Brufh-maker*, High-ftreet.
Span, Samuel and John, *Merchants*, Princes-ftreet, Counter on the Quay.
Span, Samuel, Efq. Clifton.
Sparrun, Thomas, *Paftry-cook*, Montague-ftreet.
Spearin, James, *Malifter*, Milk-ftreet.
Speed, John, Gent. Hotwell-road.
Spencer, Luke, *Lighter-mafter*, Ditto.
Spencer, Richard, *Mason*, North-ftreet.
Spencer, William, *Mason*, Redcliff-ftreet.
Spiring, L. L. *Mufic-feller*, Union-ftreet
Spiring and Co. *Seedsmen, &c.* Caftle-ftreet.
Spiring, Edward, fen. *Nursery and Seedsman*, Upper Eafton
Springer, Jofiah, *Mathematical Inftrument-maker*, Clare-ftreet.
Springer, William, *Optician*, Charles's-ftreet.
Sprud, James, *Stocking-maker*, 38, Old-market.
Spurlock, Abraham, *Taylor*, St. Auguftines-place.
Spurlock, Mary, *Paper-fhop*, Thomas-ftreet.
Spurrier, William, *Cabinet-maker*, Thomas-ftreet.
Spurrier, William, *Taylor*, Temple-ftreet.
Squier, George, Gent. Bedminfter-caufeway.
Stacy, Mary, *Lodging-houfe*, 7, Duke-ftreet.
Stagg, James, *Hair-dreffer*, Old-market.
Stallaway, Charles, *Tea-dealer*, Upper Maudlin-lane.
Stalleraffe, Martin, *French Stay-maker*, College-green.
Standfaft and Brittan, *Shoemakers*, St. James's church-yard.
Stanley, Thomas, *Carpenter*, 8, St. James's-parade.
Stanfbury, Jofeph, *Mufician*, Caftle-ditch.
Stanfell, William, *Hat-maker and Furrier*, Caftle-ftreet.
Stansfield, James and Co. *Snuff-manufacturers*, Ditto.
Star and Co. *Linen-drapers*, Bath-ftreet.
Stedman, Henry, *Watch-cafe maker*, Thomas-ftreet.
Stenfon, Thomas, *Hofier*, 17, Union-ftreet.
Stephens, Edward, *Plumber*, Milk-ftreet.
Stephens, Henry, *Old Queen Mary*, Quay.
Stephens, Robert and Co. *Gun-makers*, Ditto.
Stephens, William, *Worehouseman*, Wine-ftreet.
Stephens, John, *Broker*, 34, Maryport-ftreet
Stephens, James, *Cabinet-maker*, 53, Caftle-ftreet.
Stephens, Richard, Efq. Hotwell-road.
Stephens, William, *Maft-maker*, Ditto.

Stephens.

Stephens, Thomas, *Carpenter*, Stoney-hill.
Stephens, Elizabeth, *Ladies' Boarding-school*, Upper Maudlin-lane.
Stephens, John, *Taylor*, 59, St. Michaels-hill.
Stephens, Mary, *Milliner*, 14, Charles's-street.
Stephens, William and Co. *Maltsters, Brewers, and Cyder-merchants*, Wilder-street.
Stephens, Thomas, *Music-seller*, Narrow Wine-street.
Stephens, John, *Three Tuns*, Great Ann-street.
Stevens, Mr. James, Bedminster.
Stevens, Cave, and Co. *Flint and Crown-glass manufacturers*, Redcliff-backs.
Stevens, Cave, and Co. *Crown-glass manufacturers*, Thomas-str.
Steward, Alexander, *Custom-house officer*, Wells's-street.
Stewart, Mark, *Goldsmith*, Nicholas-street.
Stewart, John, *Custom-house officer*, Park.
Stuff, John, *Haberdasher*, Union-street.
Stunton, Philip, *Lodging-house*, Lower College-street.
Stock, Thomas, *Grocer*, Bath-street.
Stockdale, Peregrine, *Woollen-draper*, 42, High-street.
Stockdale, Thomas, *Merchant*, 3, Somerset-street.
Stockham, William, *Baker*, 22, Castle-street.
Stockham, Henry, *Baker*, Bedminster.
Stocking, Thomas, *Tyler and Plaisterer*, Limekiln-lane.
Stockwell, William, *Basket-maker*, Peter-street.
Stokes, Capt. Thomas, Southwell-street.
Stokes, John, *Butcher*, Bedminster.
Stokes, Richard, *Butcher*, Bedminster-causeway.
Stone, Francis, *Goldsmith, &c.* Bristol-bridge.
Stone, Charles, *Cornfactor*, St. Michaels-hill.
Stone, James, *Pawnbroker*, 6, Old-market.
Stone, Sarah, *Bell*, West-street.
Stone, James, *Horse-shoe and Talbot*, Ditto.
Stone, James, *Swan*, Temple-street.
Stone, John, *Carpenter*, Frog-lane.
Stonehouse, Rev. Sir James, Bart. Hotwell-parade.
Stoner, Ambrose, *Linen-draper*, 19, High-street.
Storther, William, *Accomptant*, Southwell-street.
Stott, George, *Merchant*, Tower-street.
Stratton, Sarah, *Pastry-cook*, St. Michaels-hill.
Stratton, Richard, *Wheelwright*, Milk-street.
Stratton, William, *Hair-dresser*, Broad-mead.
Streeter, Uriah, *Pastry-cook*, Thunderbolt-street.
Strickland, Roger, *Tea-dealer*, Castle-ditch.
Strickland, Jacob, *Joiner*, Baldwin-street.
Stringer, Gabriel, *Carver and Gilder*, St. Johns-bridge.

Stroud,

Stroud, James, *Glazier*, Narrow Wine-ftreet.
Stubs, John, *Ironmonger*, Newfoundland-ftreet.
Stuckey, Joel, *Shoe and Saddle-warehoufe*, Redcliff-ftreet.
Studley,   *Merchant*, 19, College-green.
Sturge, Jofeph, *Mufician*, Marlborough-ftreet.
Sturling, Sarah, *Ship and Pilot*, Quay.
Stych, John, *Linen-draper*, 22, Union-ftreet.
Summers, James, *Engineer*, Lawrence-hill.
Suple, Francis and Son, *Linen-drapers*, Union-ftreet.
Sutton, Capt. George, Park-row.
Sutton, John, *Ivory Turner*, Corn-ftreet.
Sutton, James, *Hooper*, 91, Redcliff-ftreet.
Swan, Abraham, *Lock-fmith*, Horfe-fair.
Swanton and Weare, *Milliners*, Rofemary-ftreet.
Swayne, Walter, *Ironmonger*, Wine-ftreet.
Sweetman, Sufannah, *Baker*, 47, Princes-ftreet.
Symes and Kindon, *Brick-makers*, Redclift.
Symes, Richard, Efq. St Michaels-hill.
Symonds, John, *Lamb and Flag*, Temple-ftreet.
Symonds, William, *Accomptant*, Broad-mead, office at Mr.
          Marklove's, Small-ftreet.
Symons, Butler, *Wine and Brandy-merchant*, King-fquare.

T

Tagart and Green, *Linen-drapers*, Union-ftreet.
Taglie, William, *Carpenter*, Bedminfter.
Tandy, John, *Tide Surveyor*, Bedminfter-caufeway
Tanner, John, *Tanner*, River-ftreet.
Tanner, James, *Fountain*, Pithay.
Tanner, Mark, *Hallier*, Hotwell-road.
Tanner, George, *Working-cutler*, Maryport-ftreet.
Tanner, John, *Breeches-maker*, Ditto.
Tanner, L. *Perfumer*, 32, Wine-ftreet.
Tapfcott, William, Gent. Stokes-croft.
Taylor, Thomas, *Sugar Loaf*, Rofemary-ftreet.
Taylor, George, *Queen's-head*, Quay.
Taylor and Tomkins, *Linen-drapers*, 41, High-ftreet.
Taylor, William, *Baker*, 18, Broad-ftreet.
Taylor, John, *Leather-dreffer*, 10, Maryport-ftreet.
Taylor, Thomas, *Accomptant*, College-ftreet
Taylor, Philip, *Staffordfhire-warehoufe*, Quay-ftreet.
Taylor, Daniel, *Baker*, Hotwell-road.
Taylor, Thomas, *Gardener*, Fort-lane.

Taylor, S *Lodging-house*, Horfield-lane.
Taylor, Nicholas, *Baker*, Lewins-mead.
Taylor, Martha, *Plumber*, Baldwin-ftreet.
Taylor, Jofeph, *Maltfter*, St Philips-place.
Taylor, William, *Bell*, Broad-ftreet
Taylor, Robert, *Three Black-birds*, Temple-backs.
Taylor, Capt. Cob, 10, Guinea-ftreet
Taylor, Thomas, *Brick-maker*, 1, Somerfet-fquare.
Taylor, Sarah, *Shipwright's-arms*, Redcliff-ftreet.
Taylor, William, *Gardener*, Bedminfter.
Taylor, John, Efq. Redland.
Teaft, Sydenham, *Ship-builder*, Wapping
Teed, Thomas, *Mariner*, under the Bank
Telphord, William, *Mason's-arms*, Bedminfter.
Terrell, William, *Flax-drefer*, Back
Thatcher, John, *Il fut*, Redcliff-ftreet
Thierv, Richard, *Stocking-manufaturer*, Bedminfter.
Thinbeck, John, *Ready-made Linen-warehoufe*, Bath-ftreet.
Thomas, William, *Hofier*, Broad-ftreet.
Thomas, Thomas, *Brandy-merchant*, Ditto.
Thomas, John, *Shoemaker*, Maryport-ftreet.
Thomas, John, *Milliner*, Union-ftreet.
Thomas, Peter, *Shoemaker*, 5, Peter-ftreet.
Thomas and Clark, *Linen-drapers*, 9, Ditto.
Thomas, Timothy, *Tallow-chandler*, Caftle-ftreet.
Thomas, William, *Taylor*, 21, Ditto.
Thomas, John, *Crown*, Hotwells.
Thomas, Morgan, *Lodging-houfe*, Clifton.
Thomas, John, *Lodging-houfe*, Hotwell-road
Thomas, William, *Tyler and Plaifterer*, Ditto
Thomas, David, *Taylor*, Limekiln-lane.
Thomas, John, *Grocer*, St. Auguftines-back.
Thomas, John, *Accomptant*, Stoney-hill.
Thomas, John, *Carpenter*, St. Michaels-hill.
Thomas, Thomas, *Tyler and Plaifterer*, Lower Maudlin-lane.
Thomas, C L *Supervifor*, Montague-ftreet.
Thomas, Evan, *Accomptant*, Bloomfbury-buildings.
Thomas, Jofeph, *Painter*, Balloon-court, Wilder-ftreet.
Thomas, John, *Wine-merchant*, Taylor's-court.
Thomas and Proffer, *Bafket-makers*, Chriftmas-ftreet.
Thomas, John, *Cabinet-maker*, Narrow Wine-ftreet.
Thomas, John, *Accomptant*, Caftle-green
Thomas, James, *Taylor*, Old-market
Thomas, William, *Waterman's-arms*, Back-ftreet.
Thomas, Edward, *Malman*, Little Ann-ftreet.

Thomas

Thomas and Ames, *Maltsters*, St Philips-place.
Thomas, John, *Grocer*, Bridge-parade.
Thomas, Theophilus, *Tide Surveyor*, Somerset-square.
Thomas, Hannah, *Pawnbroker*, Redcliff-hill.
Thomas, Samuel, *Leather-dresser*, Quakers-friers.
Thomas, Philip, *Crown and Pipes*, Broad-mead.
Thomas, John, *Tyler and Plaisterer*, Trenchard-lane.
Thomas, Lewis, *Accomptant*, 5, Norfolk-street.
Thornell, John, *Mariner*, Back-street.
Thompson, *Lodging-house*, Queen-square.
Thompson, M. *Perfumer*, Castle-street.
Thompson, James, *Coach and Horses*, Currant-lane.
Thompson, George, *Perfumer*, Hotwells.
Thompson, Capt. William, 29, College-street.
Thompson, Capt. James, 2, Wells's-street.
Thompson, Thomas, *Maltster*, Little Ann-street.
Thompson, Richard, *Breeches-maker*, Temple-street.
Thompson, Elizabeth, *Coffee-house*, Exchange.
Thorban, Thomas, *Ship*, Limekiln-lane.
Thorne, Thomas, *Haberdasher*, Bridge-street.
Thorne, Romain Joseph, *Accomptant*, Southwell-street.
Thorne, George, *Silk-mercer*, Marlborough-street.
Thrall, Jacob, *Fruiterer*, 28, Bridge-street.
Thriffel, Edward, *Roap-maker*. Stapleton-road.
Tilladam, William, *Shoemaker*, West-street.
Tilly, William, *Hooper*, Old-market.
Timberman, William, *Hooper*, Counter-slip.
Tinkler, William, *Corn-chandler*, Lamb-street.
Tirer, Richard, *Tin-plate worker*, St James's church-yard.
Tobin and Pinney, *West India-merchants*, Great Georges-street
Tobin, James, Esq *Merchant*, St. James's-square.
Todd, James, *Breeches-maker*, 86, Castle-street.
Tombs, Richard, *Ship-builder*, Deans-marsh.
Tomlinson, T. P. *Accomptant*, Wilder-street.
Tomlinson and Cator, *Maltsters*, St Philips-plain.
Tommas, John, *Lime-burner*, Limekiln-dock.
Tong, Benjamin, *Shoemaker*, Quay.
Tovey, George, *Brush-maker*, Narrow Wine-street.
Tovey, Thomas, *Patent Coach-lamp maker*, Stokes-croft.
Tovey, William, *Baker*, Baptist-mills.
Tower, Joseph, *Shoemaker*, Lawrence-hill.
Townsend, Sarah, *Queen's-head*, Barton.
Toye, Henry, *Linen-draper*, High-street.
Tozer, Arthur, *Tobacconist*, Maryport-street.
Tozer, John, *Accomptant*, Castle-ditch.

Tozer,

er, Francis, *Tyler and Plaisterer*, Thomas-ftreet.

er, Arthur, *Porter-brewer*, Bath-ftreet.

app, William, *Accomptant*, Guinea-ftreet.

att, James, *Taylor*, Cathay.

ngg, Jofeph and Co *Tobacconifts*, 49, Caftle-ftreet.

npp, John, *Taylor and Salesman*, Thomas-ftreet

npp and Jenkins, *Salesmen*, Quay.

npp, Daniel, *Sugar-loaf*, Milk-ftreet.

rodenbury, Capt. William, 5, College-ftreet.

otman, William, *Woollen-draper*, Clare-ftreet.

oughton and Hodgetts, *Coventry-warehoufe*, Broad-ftreet

rowbridge, William, *Butcher*, Redcliff-hill.

rufted, Edward, *Ship-rigger*, 3, Pipe-lane.

rucker, James, *Farrier*, Limekiln-lane and Hotwell-road.

rucker, Mary, *Grocer*, Lower Maudlin-lane

rucker, Benjamin, *Carpenter*, Portland-ftreet.

rucker, William, *Wheat Sheaf*, Queen-ftreet.

rucker, Sufannah, *Grocer*, 26, Redcliff ftreet.

rucker, Thomas, *Hay-weigher*, Broad-mead.

rucketts and Fletcher, *Wholesale Grocers and Fruit-merchants*, Corn-ftreet.

Tucketts and Fletcher, *Sugar-refners*, Bath-ftreet.

Tugwell, Minchin, Gent. 22, Montague-ftreet.

Tulk, Thomas, *Glazier*, Redcliff-hill

Tully, George, *Furrier*, Maryport-ftreet.

Turnbull, William, *Land Surveyor*, Old-market.

Turner, Richard, *Mealman*, 35, Bridge-ftreet

Turner, Jofeph, *Hooper*, Marfh-ftreet.

Turner, William, Efq. Redcliff-hill.

Turner, William, *Merchant*, Lodge-ftreet.

Turnpenny, John, *Painter and Glazier*, Bridge-ftreet.

Twitty, T. H. *Hooper*, Hoft-ftreet.

Tyler, Mary, *Lodging-houfe*, College-ftreet.

Tyler, William, *Prince Frederick*, Lewins-mead

Tyler, William, *Dealer in Spirits*, Nicholas-ftreet.

Tyndall, Power, and Townfend, *Dry-falters*, Wine-ftreet

Tyndall, Thomas, Efq Clifton-hill

U and V

Underwood, William, Gent. Lower Eafton.

Underwood, James, *Wool-ftapler*, Thomas-ftreet

Urch, Thomas, *Baker*, St. Auguftines-back.

Uther, J. and T. *Wholefale Linen-drapers*, Wine ftreet.

L

Vagg,

Vagg, John, *Three Tuns*, Old King-street.
Vanderhorst, Elias, Esq. Queen-square.
Vandyke, Philip, *Portrait-painter*, St. Augustines-back,
Vandyke, Mrs.   *Toy and Perfume-shop*, Ditto.
Varlow, Samuel, *Hair-dresser*, North-street.
Vaughan and Co. *Timber-merchants*, Back.
Vaughan, James, Esq Great Georges-street.
Vaughan, T. G. *Merchant*, Small-street.
Vaughan, Baugh, and Co. *Linen-merchants*, Ditto.
Vaughan, Richard, Esq. St. Michaels-hill.
Vaughan, James, *Accomptant*, Marlborough-street.
Vaughan, Philip, *Golden Lyon*, Horse-fair.
Vaughan, John, *Maremaid*, Lewins-mead.
Vaughans, Baker, and Co. *Bankers*, Corn-street.
Veal,   *Lodging-house*, 3, Hotwell-parade.
Vernam, William, *Wine-merchant*, St. Augustines-place.
Vernam, Robert, *Brightsmith*, Counter-slip.
Verncomb, Mary, *Cheese-factor*, St. Stephens-street.
Vigor, Mrs. Frances, Redcliff-parade.
Vigors, Jane, `King's-arms`, King-street.
Vigurs and Bowen, *Woollen-drapers*, High-street.
Viner, Christopher, *Hat-maker*, 7, Ditto.
Viner, E. W. *Broker*, Corn-street.
Viner, Ann, *Tobacco-pipe manufacturer*, Host-street.
Viner, Hester, *Lodging-house*, Durdham-down.
Viner, Isaac, *Leather-dresser*, 2, Bridge-street.
Viner, Isaac, *Glover and Undertaker*, High-street.
Viney, Joseph, *Cabinet-maker*, Thomas-street.
Vining, Thomas, *Grocer*, Bridge-parade.
Vinson, Nicholas, *Lamb and Lark*, Tower-street.
Vizer, Robert, *Accomptant*, St. Stephen-street.
Vowles, John, *Baker*, Earl-street.
Vowles, Joseph, *Taylor*, Castle-green.

W

Wade, Josiah and Co. *Linen-drapers*, Wine-street.
Wade, Capt. Peter, Orchard-street
Wadham and Son, *Glaziers*, Host-street.
Wadham, Ricketts, and Co *Flint-glass manufacturers*, Without
        Temple-gate.
Wadley, Edmund, *Hair-dresser and Perfumer*, St. Augustines-back
Wady, William, *Wetch-maker*, Lower Maudlin-lane.
Wady, John, *Dentist*, Ditto.

Wagg,

Wigg, Abraham, Gent. Charles's-ftreet.
Wait, Daniel and Sons, *Grocers*, Broad-ftreet.
Wait, John, *Dry-falter*, Caftle-ftreet.
Waldo, Jofeph, *Merchant*, Unity-ftreet.
Walker, Robert, *Dancing-mafter*, College-green.
Walker, Capt. James, Culver-ftreet.
Walker, Thomas, *Taylor*, Steep-ftreet.
Walker, Thomas, Efq. Redland.
Wall and Daniel, *Tea-dealers and China-men*, Wine-ftreet.
Wall, John, *Auctioneer*, Ditto.
Wall, Thomas, *Brewer*, Montague-ftreet.
Wallis, Thomas, *Shoemaker*, Gay-ftreet.
Wallis, James, *Baker*, Frog-lane.
Walters, Henry, *King's-head*, Wine-ftreet.
Walters, William, *Horn-worker*, St. Auguftines-back.
Walters, William, Efq. Park.
Walters, Howell, *Accomptant*, Caftle-green.
Walters, William, *Three Horse-fhoes*, Old-market.
Walters, William, *Glass-houfe*, Lawrence-hill.
Wanklin, William, *Diftiller*, King-ftreet.
Ward, Elizabeth, *Lodging-houfe*, Princes-ftreet.
Ward, John, *Tallow-chandler*, Caftle-ftreet.
Ward, John, Gent St Michaels-hill.
Waring, John, *Merchant*, Queen-fquare and Quay.
Waring and Frank, *Ironmongers*, Bridge-ftreet.
Waring, Thomas, Gent. 48, Montague-ftreet.
Warn, Samuel, *Writing-mafter*, Redcliff-ftreet.
Warner, Henry, *Bafket-maker*, Maryport-ftreet
Warner, William, *Bookseller*, Bridewell-lane.
Wafbrough and Son, *Organifts*, College-green.
Wafbrough, William, *Brafs-founder*, Narrow Wine-ftreet.
Wafher, Dorothy, *Ship-chandler*, Princes-ftreet.
Wafon, John James, *Merchant*, Queen-fquare.
Waters, Jofeph, *Horn-worker*, Redcliff-ftreet.
Waters, Thomas, *Butcher*, Bedminfter.
Waters, William, Gent. Ditto.
Watkin, *Shoemaker*, Hotwells.
Watkins, James, *Mariner*, Montague-ftreet.
Watkins, John, *Tyler and Plaifterer*, Horfe-fair.
Watkins, William, *Shoemaker*, St. James's church-yard.
Watkins, Ann, *Milliner*, Ditto.
Watkins, John, *Hair-dreffer*, John-ftreet.
Watkins, Robert, *Currier*, Redcliff-ftreet.
Watkins, Evan. *Excise-officer*, Somerfet-place.
Watkins, Evan, *Bell and Compaffes*, Merchant-ftreet.

Watkins,

Watkins, William, *Tide Surveyor*, Rennison's-bath.
Watts, William, *Hoster*, 26, High-street.
Watts, Nathaniel, *Grocer*, Castle-street.
Watts, William, Gent. 14, Sion-row.
Watts, William, *Accomptant*, 5, Denmark-street.
Watts, Samuel, *Accomptant*, Park.
Watts, Samuel, *Lead-merchant*, Guinea-street.
Watts, William, *Lead-merchant*, Redcliff-hill.
Watts and Co *Patent Shot-manufacturers*, Ditto.
Wayne, William, *Dealer in Spirits*, Peter-street.
Weall, George, *Accomptant*, Temple-backs.
Weare, William, Esq. Brunswick-square.
Weare, John Fisher, *Merchant*, Queen-square.
Weaver, Francis, *Tallow-chandler*, Castle-street.
Weaver, E. *Lodging-house*, Albermarle-row.
Weaver, William, *Malt shovel*, Jacob-street.
Weaver, Isaac, *Brandy-merchant*, Redcliff-street.
Webb, Joseph, *Mason*, Milk-street
Webb, James, *Glover and Undertaker*, Broad-street.
Webb, Capt. William, Quay-lane.
Webb, William, *Perish Clerk*, Clifton
Webb, Richard, *St. Augustine's Tavern*, Frog-lane.
Webb, Thomas, Esq. 10, Paul-street.
Webb, Lieut. Thomas, 3, Portland-street.
Webb, Richard, *Carpenter*, Charles's-street
Webb, Thomas, *Rule maker*, Earl-street
Webb, John, Gent Dove-street
Webb, Jacob, *Hooper*, Horse-fair
Webb, Thomas, *Pump-maker*, Ditto.
Webb, John, *Shoemaker*, St. James's-parade.
Webb, John, *Gardener*, Whitehall,
Webb, Elizabeth, *Pawnbroker*, St Philips-place.
Webb, William *Queen's head*, Bread-street.
Webb, Joseph, *Hooper*, Redcliff-street
Webb, Mary, *Hoster*, 43, Ditto.
Webb, George, *Chair-man &c*, Bedminster-causeway,
Webb, John, Esq Durdham-down.
Webber, James, *Brandy-merchant*, Milk-street
Webley, Thomas, *Fox*, Redcliff-street.
Webster, John, *Mercer*, Gay-street.
Weekes, George, *Mayor's-officer*, Marlborough-street.
Weeks, John, *Bush and Tavern*, Corn-street.
Weeks,   *Carpenter*, Denmark-street.
Welch, John, *Hooper*, Lewins-mead.
Weldy, John, *Accomptant*, Norfolk-street.

Wells,

Wells, Ortando, 17, Queen-square.
Wells, William, *Fox*, Baptist-mills.
Wenman, Hon Richard, 6, Park-street.
Were, Joseph, *Merchant*, King-square.
Werrie, John, *Brightsmith*, Peter-street.
Weson, James, *Boar's-head*, Nicholas-street.
Westcott, Martha, *Corn-chandler*, Steep-street.
Westcott, George, *Mason*, Hillgrove-street.
Westcott, William, *Dealer in Spirits*, Temple-street.
Westcott, Jasper and Co *Brass-founders, and Copper-smiths*, Red-
    cliff-street
West, Thomas, *Shoemaker*, Bedminster-causeway.
Westley, Edward, *Merchant*, Queen-square.
Weston, Thomas, *Upholder*, Philadelphia-street.
Westwood, William, *Corn-Exchange Tavern*, Quay-street.
Wetherill, William and Son, *Merchants*, Back.
Weymouth, Henry, *Carpenter*, Bedminster.
Whealer, Nathaniel, *Star and Garter*, Narrow Wine-street.
Wheeler and Dunn, *Linen-drapers*, 35, High-street.
Whiffen,   *Montague Tavern*, Kingsdown-parade.
Whitaker, Sarah, *Broker*, Thomas-street.
Whitby,   *Lodging-house*, College-street.
Whitchurch, James, *Merchant*, Oxford-street.
Whitchurch, William, *Baker*, Montague-street.
Whitchurch, Samuel, *Insurance-broker*, Exchange.
White, Charles, *Pump and Engine-maker*, Glocester-street
White, Thomas, *Pump-maker*, Milk-street
White and Collier, *Perfumers* Union-street.
White, John, *Breeches-maker*, Dolphin-street.
White, George, *Watch-maker*, Castle-street.
White, Capt. Joseph, College-street
White, Joseph, *Carpenter*, Lower-green.
White, John, *Patten-ring maker*, Marlborough-street
White, Thomas, *Shoemaker*, Bridewell-lane.
White, Richard, *Custom-house officer*, Host-street.
White, Thomas, *Basket-maker*, St John's-bridge.
White, James, *Basket-maker*, Glocester-lane
White, William, *Cabinet-maker*, St. Philips.
White, James, *Pail of Barm*, Bedminster.
Whitehead, Thomas, Esq. *Banker*, St. Michaels-hill.
Whitehouse, Samuel, *Baker*, St Philips-plain.
Whitewood, Samuel, Gent Upper Easton.
Whitford, William, *Turner*, 58, Castle-street.
Whitford, John, *Baker*, 7, Old-market
Whitlock, Mary, *Grocer*, Thomas-street.

                                        Whitrow,

Whitrow, William, *Cheese-factor*, Bridewell-lane.
Whitrow, Robert, *Accomptant*, Tower-ftreet.
Whittingham, William, *Skinner*, Pennywell-lane.
Whittuck and Ludlow, *Hatters*, Caftle-ftreet.
Whittuck, Charles, Gent. 8, Redcrofs-ftreet.
Wickland, Francis, *Dentift*, Captain Carey's-lane.
Wigan, Thomas, *Goldfmith*, Bridge-ftreet.
Wigan, Thomas and Co. *Diftillers*, &c. Jacob-ftreet
Wigan, Edward, *Ship-rigger*, Frog-lane.
Wigginton and Co. *Tobacconifts*, Back.
Wilcocks, Ann, *Lodging-houfe*, Stoney-hill.
Wilcomb, John, *Boar's-head*, Limekiln-lane.
Wilcox, Capt. Edward, Barton-ftreet.
Wilcox, John, *Merchant*, St. Philips-place.
Wilcox, Hanmer, and Co. *Starch-manufacturers*, St. Philips.
Wilcox, John, *Hat-maker*, Bedminfter.
Wildey, Matthew, *Sail-maker*, Quay.
Wildgoofe, Richard, *Lime-burner*, St. Philips-place.
Wildgoofe, John, *Shoemaker*, Redcliff-ftreet.
Wiles, Mofes, *Cuftom-houfe officer*, Kington's-buildings.
Wilks, Thomas, *Mariner*, Culver-ftreet.
Wilkins, John, *Royal Ann*, Wapping.
Willett, Jofeph, *Grocer*, Caftle-ftreet.
Willey, Thomas, *Wheat Sheaf*, Thomas-ftreet.
Williams, William, *Sadler*, Rofemary-ftreet.
Williams, Thomas, *Hair-dreffer*, Philadelphia-ftreet.
Williams, Thomas, *Malt-mill maker*, Ditto.
Williams and Hewfon, *Sadlers*, 14, Broad-ftreet.
Williams, Jofeph, *Mulberry-tree Tavern*, Ditto.
Williams, Ricketts, and Co *Tobacconifts*, Maryport-ftreet
Williams and Co. *Hat-manufacturers*, 5, Caftle-ftreet.
Williams, Sir Edward, Bart. Clifton-hill.
Williams,   *Glafs-houfe*, Hotwell-road.
Williams, William, *Excife-officer*, Ditto.
Williams, William, *Livery Stable-keeper*, Limekiln-lane.
Williams, John, *Carpenter*, Lower College-ftreet
Williams, E. R. Efq. Park-ftreet.
Williams, William, *Grocer*, Frog-lane.
Williams, Robert, *Mariner*, Stoney-hill.
Williams, Thomas, *Grocer*, Griffin-lane.
Williams, William, *Tyler and Plaifterer*, Ditto
Williams, William, *Accomptant*, Cotham-hill.
Williams, William, *Mafon*, Clarence-place.
Williams, Thomas, Gent. 16, Montague-ftreet.
Williams, Capt. Thomas, Dove-ftreet.

Williams,

Williams, Row, Efq. 23, King-fquare.
Williams, David, *Organift*, St. James's church-yard.
Williams, Charles, *Patten-maker*, Christmas-ftreet.
Williams, Thomas and Co. *Diftillers*, Narrow Wine-ftreet.
Williams, Samuel, *Cabinet-maker*, Caftle-green.
Williams, Charles, *Grocer*, Weft-ftreet.
Williams, David, *Hair-cloth maker*, Ditto.
Williams, James, *Salt-refiner*, Ditto.
Williams, Jofeph, Gent. Lawrence-hill.
Williams, Mary, *Tripe-houfe*, St. James's-back.
Williams, John, Gent. Upper Eafton.
Williams, Thomas, *George and Dragon*, Great Georges-ftreet.
Williams, William, *Lamb and Lark*, Thomas-ftreet.
Williams, William, *Cabinet-maker*, Ditto.
Williams, Robert, *Watch-maker*, Bath-ftreet.
Williams, William, *Accomptant*, Avon-ftreet.
Williams, William, *Queen's-head Inn*, Redcliff-ftreet.
Williams, Thomas, *Baker*, Ditto.
Williams, Eliza, *Dealer in Spirits*, Ditto.
Williams, James and Co. *Brandy-merchants*, Ditto.
Williams, Thomas, *Gardener*, Bedminfter.
Williams, Ifaac, *Lamb*, Ditto
Williams, Thomas, *Wheelwright*, Red-hill.
Williams, Richard, *Pump-maker*, Broad-mead.
Williams, Daniel, *Writing-mafter*, Corn-market-lane.
Willis and Sheppard, *Stocking-manufacturers*, Wine-ftreet.
Willis, Edward, *Hofier and Glover*, High-ftreet.
Willis, Francis, *Auctioneer*, Bridge-ftreet.
Wills, John, *Brazier*, Caftle-ftreet.
Wilmot, Thomas, *Merchant*, Quay and Queen-fquare.
Wilmot, Thomas, *Carpenter*, Thomas-ftreet.
Wilmot, Charles, *Mafon*, Temple-backs.
Wilmot, Samuel, *Maltfter*, Redcliff-ftreet.
Wilfon, Capt. James, 4, Paul-ftreet
Wilfon, Mary, *Grocer*, 26, Old-market.
Wiltfhire, Sarah, *Adam and Eve*, Lewins-mead.
Wiltfhire, Thomas, *Brafs-founder*, Thomas ftreet
Wilway, George, *Cabinet-maker*, Broad-mead.
Wind, William, *Organ-builder*, Bridewell-bridge.
Windfor, Thomas, *Cuftom-houfe officer*, Newgate-ftreet.
Wingate and Co *Wool-ftaplers*, Nicholas-ftreet.
Winpenny, Richard Cook, Park-ftreet.
Winter, Thomas, *Vintner*, 8, Norfolk-ftreet.
Winter, John, *Horn-worker*, 61, Caftle-ftreet.
Winter, John, Gent. 6, King-fquare-avenue.

Winwood,

Winwood, Thomas, *West India broker*, 21, Queen-square, office in the Exchange.
Winwood and Protheroe, *Wrought Iron-founders*, West-street.
Winwood, John, *Iron-founder*, Cheese-lane.
Winscom, Thomas, *Excise-officer*, Castle-street.
Wife and Matthews, *Silversmiths*, Wine-street.
Wife, Thomas, *Carpenter*, Temple-street.
Withenbury, Thomas, *Mariner*, College-street.
Witherill, Robert, *Carpenter*, Old-market.
Witherly, Susannah, *King's-arms*, Baldwin-street
Withers, John, *Pawnbroker*, King-street,
Withers, Alexander, *Pawnbroker*, Barton-street
Withers, John, *Carpenter*, Lawrence-hill.
Withers, Thomas, *Shoemaker*, Redcliff-street.
Withington, Charles, *Cooper*, Montague-street
Withington, Mary, *Hair-preparer*, Broad-mead.
Withy, George, jun. *Woollen-draper and Salesman*, Castle-street
Wood, William, *Merchant*, Lower-green. *Agent to the Sun Fire office*, All-saints-lane.
Wood, William, *Taylor*, Redcliff-hill.
Woods, William, *Cabinet-maker*, Host-street.
Wood, Leighton, Esq. Kingsdown
Woodeson, Fare, *Cabinet-maker*, North-street.
Woodford, George, *Stay-maker*, Sims's-alley
Woodhouse, Elizabeth, *Granby-house*, Hotwells
Woodhouse and Co *Tobacconists*, Wine-street.
Woodland, Thomas, *Lodging-house*, College-street.
Woodland, Isaac, *Baker*, Back-street.
Woodland, James, *Chair-maker*, Great Georges-street
Woodward, James, *Wheelwright*, Bedminster.
Woodward, John, *Coach-maker*, Ditto
Woodward, Joseph, *Wheelwright*, Thomas-street.
Woodward, Sarah, *Sadler*, West-street.
Woodward, John, Gent. Horfield-lane.
Woolford, Thomas, *Butcher*, Bridewell-lane
Wools and Baily, *Ship-carver*, Quay.
Wordsworth, Samuel, *Carpenter*, Bridge-street.
Worgan and Son, *Watch-makers*, Wine-street
Worgan, Matthew, *Watch-maker*, Montague-street.
Workman, Edmund, Gent. Brunswick-square
Workman, Francis, Esq Queen's-parade
Wornell, Thomas, *Haberdasher*, High-street.
Worrall, Samuel, Esq *Distributer of Stamps*, Clifton.
Worrall, Samuel, Esq. *Town-clerk*, College-green
Worsley, James, *Hat-maker*, Broad Ware.

Wag 5

ght, Joseph, *Accomptant*, Newfoundland-ftreet.
ght, Capt. Charles, College-ftreet.
ght, Matthew, *Merchant*, St. Auguftines-back.
ght, Oldfield, *Cuftom-houfe officer*, Hoft-ftreet.
ght, William, *Cabinet-maker*, Glocefter-lane.
ght, Henry, *Cabinet maker*, 10, Bath-ftreet.
ght, John, *Sugar-refiner*, Temple-backs
ght, Philip, *Lime-burner*, Redcliff-backs.
ght, William, *Horfe and Jockey*, Broad-mead.
yatt, Anthony, *Baker*, Broad Ware.
ld, George, *Accomptant*, Bedminfter-parade.
yman and Clark, *Compofition-ornament manufacturer*, Broad-
mead.

Y

Yandal, John Shawland, *Accomptant*, Lower College-ftreet
Yandal, Thomas, *Wine-cooper*, Caftle-ditch.
Yarworth, William, *Wine-merchant*, Back.
Yearfley, Ann, *Public Library*, 4, Hotwell-crefcent.
Yeates and Peters, *Maltfters*, Without Temple-gate.
Yeates,   *Grocer*, Durdham-down.
Yem, Ann, *Bell*, Hilgrove-ftreet.
Yeo, John, *Ink-powder, and Liquid-blue manufacturer*, Peter-ftr.
Yeo, Thomas, *Bear Inn*, Hotwell-road.
York, Thomas, *Butcher*, Redcliff-ftreet
Young, Charles, *Merchant*, 14, Park-ftreet.
Young, Sarah, *White Hart*, Lewins-mead.
Young, Jofeph and Edward, *Millers*, Ditto.
Young, Edward, *Cornfactor*, Ditto.

Regulation of the POSTS at BRISTOL.

London - Goes out every afternoon (except Saturday) at 4 o'clock.
    —Arrives every morning, (except Monday) about noon.
Bath - - - Goes out every morning at 7, and arrives about 9 or 10
    in the evening
Exeter and Weftward, Goes out every morning between 9 and 10,
    and arrives every evening between 5 and 7.
Birmingham, &c. Northward, Goes out every evening at 7, and
    arrives every morning between 7 and 9.
          M   *Portfmouth,*

Portſmouth, Chicheſter, Saliſbury, &c. Goes out every morning at and arrives every evening between 9 and 11.

Cirenceſter, Oxford, &c Goes out every morning at 8, and arriw every evening about 6 or 7.

Milford Haven and South Wales, Goes out and arrive every d about noon.

The *Iriſh* Mail is made up every day except Monday, and let ters from *Ireland* may be expected to arrive every day about noon except Monday.

Foreign Letters diſpatched from *Briſtol* twice a week or oftener

Letters from all Parts, may be put into the Poſt-office at any time, but ſhould be delivered at leaſt half an hour before the Mail is made up.

PENNY POST OFFICE ſettled and eſtabliſhed by his Majeſty's Poſt Maſter General the 3d July, 1793; and offices are opened for the receipt of letters and packets, (not exceeding four ounces weight,) from 7 in the morning till 9 at night, at the following places, viz.

Mr. COOPER's, Grocer, corner of *Park ſtreet, College-green*

Mr. TUSTIN's, Grocer, *St. Michael's-hill.*

Mr. BROWN's, Taylor and Habit-maker, No. 5, near the *Lamb, Broad-mead.*

Miſs JEFFERY's, Milliner, *Old-market.*

Mrs. JONES's, Grocer, *Thomas-ſtreet.*

The NEW INN, *Dowry-ſquare, Hotwells.*

And CLIFTON HOTEL, at *Clifton.*

And alſo at the principal POST OFFICE, near the *Exchange,* from whence deliveries will be made to all parts of the City and ſuburbs, (including the Hotwells and Clifton) three times a day, viz. half paſt eight in the morning, twelve at noon, and half paſt five in the afternoon; before which time letters ſhould be put into the above offices, in order to be ſent by the earlieſt conveyance,— for which One Penny will be charged in the City, and Two-pence for the ſuburbs, and places within the limits of the penny poſt delivery.

Letters intended for the general poſt for *London and all parts of the kingdom,* may, on payment of one penny with them, be put into any of the receiving houſes, from whence they will be conveyed to the principal office at the proper times.

Letter carriers will be diſpatched regularly every day (Sundays excepted) with the letters to and from *Durdham-down, Stoke, Weſtbury, Henbury, Shirehampton,* and *Pill;* to *Stapleton, Frenchay, Downend, Hambrook,* and *Winterbourn;* and alſo to *Briſlington* and *Keynſham,* and to other places.

CUSTOM

CUSTOM-HOUSE, QUEEN-SQUARE.

Collector, John Powell, Efq.

His Clerks, Thomas Andrewes, Jeffe Barrett, T Abbott

Comptroler, Patrick Brydone, Efq.

Deputy-Comptroler, Cha. Harford, Efq

His Clerk, John Jones.

Cuftomer outwards and inwards, Anthony Palmer Collings, Efq.

His Clerks, James Mounfher, John Peters, William Jordan.

Examiner, William Williams.

Cheque Clerk, and Receiver of Grenwich and Briftol Hofpitals, Cornelius Gillam.

Jerquer, vacant.

Receiver of the Prisage, of the Holms, and Small Lights, Thomas Rothley, Efq.

Landing Surveyors, Henry Cafamajor, Wm. Tucker, James Edwards, one vacant.

King's-waiters, Thomas James, Jofiah Taylor, Fra. Greville, William Berrow.

Deputy King's-waiters, William Baynton, Robert King Bird, Cha Camplin, Tho Haynes.

Land-waiters, William Jolleff, Rich. Jenkins, Geo Rackfter, John Hill, Edw. Morgan, Geo. Ebbery Thomas, Carter Stiles, Nathan. Windey, Rich. Annefby Ellifon, Rich Colfton, three vacant.

Coaft-officer, William Reeve.

Patent-Searcher, Tho. Crawford, Efq.

Deputy Patent Searchers, Tho. Farr Ellifon, John Cha. Stuart.

Comptroling Searchers, Edw. P. Chamberlaine, Tho Hull.

Houfekeeper, Cath. Nicholls

Tide Surveyors, John Tandy, E. Nicholls, Samuel Fear, Theophilus Thomas.

Superintendent of the Weighing Porters, Thomas Miles.

EXCISE-OFFICE, QUEEN-SQUARE.

Collector, John Davis, Efq.

1ft Clerk, Alexander Duncan.

2d Clerk, Hugh Jones.

3d Clerk, Thomas Morris.

SUPERVISORS.

Firft Diftrict, Thomas Clement.

Second, John Pratt.

Third, Vincent Kenney.

Fourth, William Jarman.

Fifth, Thomas Payne.

Firft Diftillery Surveyor, James Graham.

Second, John Hadden.

Land Surveyor, William Snell.

Tide Surveyors, Tho. Chriftopher, William Jones.

Port-guager, Nath. Radmore.

Warehoufe-keeper, William South.

Bonded Rum Locker, Sam. Frefhwater.

Export Surveyor, David Jones.

TOBACCO WAREHOUSES.

Firft Excife Warehoufe-keeper, B. Dickenfon

Second ditto, William Barley.

PERMIT-OFFICE, *Thomas-ftr.*

Writers, John Lowe, James Dore, Evan Bevan,

PERMIT-OFFICE, *Peter-ftreet.*
Writers, Abr. Hare, E. Watkins, Jof. Awbrey, Hen. Stambury, Rich. Weftrope, Jere. Challenger, John Beffem.

Salt-Office, *St. Auguftines-bac*
Collector, Wm. Richmond, Efq
Surveying-officer, E. B. Grainge
Affiftant-officer, John Smith
Officers, T. Fitchett, W. Harn

THE INFIRMARY.

Edw. Afh, Efq. *Treafurer.*
PHYSICIANS.
James Plomer, M. D.
John Wright, M. D.
William Moncrieffe, M D
Edward Long Fox, M. D.
SURGEONS.
Godfrey Lowe.

John Padmore Noble.
Morgan Yeatman.
Jofeph Metford.
Robert Jones Allard.
Tho. Webb Dyer, *Apothecary.*
John Jordan Palmer, *Secretary.*
Jane Simmons, *Matron.*
Rev. Thomas Johns, *Chaplain.*

HACKNEY COACHES.

Owners of the coaches to take out an annual licence, and each coach to have the number belonging to it affixed in three different places, viz. on the pannel of each door, and on the pannel behind

The coaches to be at their ftands (if not hired) from 9 o'clock in the morning till 11 in the evening.

The following are the Fares to be taken when hired by Time or Diftance, viz:

	s.	d
For any time not exceeding 3 qrs of an hour - - - - - -	1	0
——————————————— an hour - - - - - -	1	6
————— 20 minutes from the firft hour - - - - - - - -	0	6
For the diftance of 1 mile and a quarter from the ftand the coach is called from - - - - - - - - - - - - - -	1	0
For the diftance of 2 miles - - - - - - - - - - - - - -	1	6
Every half mile further or lefs diftance - - - - - - - - -	0	6

If any difpute arife concerning the diftance, the ground to be meafured, if found to be as great as the driver charged for, the cofts of meafuring to be paid by the perfons refufing to pay the diftance; if lefs, the driver to pay the cofts of meafurement

Drivers (if not hired) being called, and refufing to go any diftance not exceeding 10 miles, or exacting more than their fares, or ufing any abufive language, incur a penalty of 20s. and the like fum for any other breach of the above regulations, on complaint made at the Council-houfe.

The

The following are the number of Coaches, and places where they are appointed to ſtand.

1 in Wine-ſtreet.
1 in High-ſtreet.
1 in the Old-market.
1 in James's-barton.
1 in Avenue-ſtreet, Stokes-croft.
1 in King-ſquare.
1 in College-green.
1 on St Auguſtines-back.
2 on the Quay.
2 in the Avenue leading from Clare-ſtreet to St. Stephen's Church.
2 in Princes-ſtreet.
2 on Redcliff-hill.
2 in Queen-ſquare.
2 in Old King-ſtreet.

COACHES FROM BRISTOL.

BUSH-TAVERN, Corn-ſtreet. (John Weeks,)

London—A light poſt-coach every day, a quarter before 2 o'clock
Birmingham—A poſt-coach every morning at 4; alſo a mail coach every Tueſday, Thurſday, and Sunday evenings, at 7
Oxford—A poſt-coach every morning (except Sunday) at 6
Exeter—A poſt-coach every Tueſday, Thurſday, and Saturday, mornings, at 6 o'clock
Weymouth—A poſt-coach every Monday, Wedneſday, and Friday mornings at 5
Portſmouth—A poſt-coach every, Tueſday, Thurſday, and Saturday, morning at 4
Bath—Poſt-coaches every morning at 4, 6, 9, and 11; and in the afternoon at 4 o'clock
Auſt-paſſage—A poſt-coach every morning at 8

RUMMER-TAVERN, All-ſaints-lane.

London—A mail-coach every day, at 4 o'clock in the afternoon; alſo a balloon-coach every afternoon, at 2 o'clock.
Wales—A mail-coach, every day, 12 o'clock at noon.
Birmingham—A mail coach every evening at 7 o'clock
Bath—A mail-coach every morning at 8 o'clock; alſo a coach every afternoon, at 4 o'clock

WHITE-HART-INN, Broad-ſtreet. (George Poſton.)

London—A coach in one day, every morning, at 4 o'clock.
Birmingham—A coach every morning (Sundays excepted) at 4 o'clock; alſo a mail-coach every evening, at 7 o'clock
Gloceſter—A coach every morning, at 8 o'clock, (Sund. excep.)
Exeter—A coach every Monday, Wedneſday, and Friday mornings, at 6
Bath—A coach every morning at 9 o'clock, and 4 in the afternoon.

POPE's

POPE's HEAD & PELICAN, Thomas-ſtreet. (Joſeph Pope)
London—A coach every afternoon, at half paſt one o'clock.—
☞ Families accommodated at their own hours as uſual
Bath—Coaches every day, at 9 o'clock in the morning, and 2
and 4 in the afternoon

SHIP, Small-ſtreet.

Bath—Coaches every morning, at 9 and 10 o'clock, and every
afternoon at 4 and 6 o'clock.

WHITE-LION, Broad-ſtreet. (Thomas Luce)

London—A coach in two days, ſets out Tueſdays, Thurſdays, and
Saturdays, at 7 o'clock in the morning.

GREYHOUND, Broad-mead. (Martha Cooper)

Hambrook—A coach, Tueſdays and Fridays, goes out at 10
o'clock in the morning, and returns at 6 o'clock in the evening,
and ſets out again the ſame evening for Hambrook.

WAGGONS, &c.

HARDING's Warehouſe, Elbroad-ſtreet.

Abingdon, Broughton, Clenvill, Eaſtleach, and all places adjacent,
in Thurſ. out Frid. John Simpſon.
Aſhbury, Blonſdown, Chalton, Cricklade, Highworth and all places adjacent, in Frid. out Sat. Joſeph Hirons.
Coventry and Leiceſter, through Sodbury, Tetbury and Cirenceſter, to Warwick and places adjacent, in Sat. out Mon. John
Howes,
Gloceſter, Cambridge, Lincoln, Northampton, Nottingham, Rut-
land, and Yorkſhires, in Thurſ. out Frid. Sly and Rappaz.

CARPENTER and Co. Old-market.

For London, with a guard, ſet out every Wed. and Sat. at noon,
arrive at the *White-bear, Baſinghall-ſtreet,* every Wed. and Sat.
morning, return from thence every Sun. and Wed. evenings,
arrive at Bath and Briſtol every Wed. and Sat. mornings.

WALTER WILTSHIRE's, Peter-ſtreet.

London Flying Waggons, with a guard, in and out every day at
noon.
Bath, every day in the week.

BUNCH of GRAPES, Thomas-ſtreet. (George Lye)

Warminſter, Briſtol, Bath and Saliſbury Waggons, every Mon.
Wed. and Frid. evenings, return to Briſtol next morning, forward

ward goods to Alresford, Dorchester, Salisbury, Southampton, &c. in and out every day. George Lye.

THREE QUEENS, Thomas-street. (Thomas Hodge)

Bath, in and out every day. Cornelius Cutler.

Bridgwater, and all places adjacent, in Mon out Tuef. A. Harne.

Froome, in Mon. and Thurf. out Tues. and Frid. Middleton and Cox.

Taunton, Exon, and all parts of the West, in Tuef. out Wed. Thomas Webber

Shepton Mallet, and places adjacent, in Tues. and Frid. out Thurs. and Mon. Joseph Webber.

Slade, Binegar, Chilcompton, &c. in and out Wed. and Frid. Penelope Feiris.

Paulton, &c. in and out every day. William Oakes.

Yatton, in and out Wed. and Sat. John Sainfbury.

THREE KINGS, Thomas-street. (John Porter)

Bath, every day. G. Castle.

Beaminster, in Tues. out Wed. William Dix.

Bradford, in and out Tues. Thurs. and Sat. —— Dowdall.

Bridport, and places adjacent, in Tues out Wed. Wm Dix.

Crewkern, in Tues. out Wed. Ditto.

Evercreech, Wincanton, &c in Mon. out Tues. Wm Slade.

Shepton Mallett, in and out Tues. and Sat. John Webb.

Salisbury, Portfmouth, &c. in and out Tues. and Frid. ——Ofborn,

Wells, in Mon. and Thur. out Tues and Frid. —— Westcott,

FROMONT and HOLBROOK's Warehouse, Broad-mead.

London Flying Waggons, to *Bloffom's-inn, Lawrence-lane, Cheapfide.* Set out every Wed and Sat afternoon, come Wed. and Sat. morning early ---Also forward goods to all parts of **England**, Scotland, Wales and Ireland

GREYHOUND, Broad-mead. (Martha Cooper)

Durfley, Glocefter, Hereford and all parts adjacent, in Tues. out Wed Edward Millard.

Chippenham, in Mon out Tues. Thomas Ruffell.

Malmfbury, and places adjacent, in and out Tues. Hen. Ratcliff.

Tetbury, in Tues and Frid out Wed. and Sat. —— Price,

Wickwar, twice a week, (days uncertain) —— Rugg.

GEORGE, Caftle-ftreet (J Cox)

Sodbury, Didmarton, Tetbury, Minchin-hampton, Nailsworth, &c in and out Wed and Frid. Thomas Gardener.

Cirencefter, in and out Tues. and Frid. —— Pagett.

Grittleton

Grittleton, Malford, &c. in and out every Tues.   Oliver Calley.

Sodbury, in and out Wed. and Sat. —— Ball.

Wickwar, in and out every Mon. a Cart. —— Taylor.

Cromall, once a week. (days uncertain) —— Scott.

BEAR, Redcliff-ſtreet. (William Coram)

Exeter, and all adjacent places, in Tues. out Wed. W. Prickman.

Bath, in and out every day. Ralph Davis.

Shaftſbury, Poole, Blandford, Wareham, &c. in and out every Mon. Davis and Foot.

Axbridge, in and out twice a week (days uncertain) William Colesworthy.

Bridgwater, in Wed. and Frid. out Mon. and Thurs. James Tamlin.

Yeovil, in Tues. out Wed. William Symonds.

Bathford, &c. in and out twice a week, (days uncertain) W Hart

Wellington, in and out every Frid. Bartholomew Hurley.

Watchet, Minehead, and all places adjacent, in Thurs out Frid. Thomas Milton

Wiveliſcomb, in and out every Tues. William Ratlett

WHITE LION, Thomas-ſtreet. (John Aſhmore)

Birmingham, Bromſgrove, Liverpool, &c. in Wed. and Sat. out Thurs. and Sun. John Aſhmore.

Bridport, in Tues. out Wed. T. Tytherleigh.

Bath, in and out every day Carpenter and Co.

Blandford, and all parts of the Iſle of Purbeck, in Mon. out Tues. William Hix.

Corſham, once a week, (days uncertain) J. Fennel.

Exeter, in Mon out Tues. Froſt and Sheppard.

Nailſworth, in Wed. out Thurs. Ditto.

Shaftſbury, once a week, (days uncertain) A. Clavey.

Exeter, (Fly) Queen-camel, Yeovil, Axminſter, Honiton, &c in and out every Thurs. E and J. Single

Melkſham and Broughton, in and out Frid. and Mon. Carpenter and Co.

Wells, and places adjacent, in Mon. and Thurs. out Thurs. and Frid. John Fuller.

RED LION, Redcliff-ſtreet. (Lewis Jenkins)

Croſs, in and out Tues. and Frid. J. Rowe.

Axbridge and Chedder, in and out every Thurs. J. Haylin.

Churchill, in and out Wed. and Sat. Wm. Croſs.

Clevedon, in and out Wed. and Sat. Mary Long.

——— in and out Wed. and Sat. Heſter Giblefs.

Langford, in and out Wed. and Sat. Wm. Croſs.

QUEEN'.

QUEEN'S-HEAD, Redcliff-ftreet. (Wm. Williams)
Langford, in and out Wed. and Sat. William Skull.
Wrington, in and out Wed. and Sat.

ANGEL, Redcliff-ftreet. (Sarah Lovell)
Banwell, twice a week, (days uncertain) John Millard
—— twice a week, (days uncertain) Jofeph Nott.

CRAB's-WELL, Temple-ftreet. (John Lifcomb)
Devizes, in Tues. Thurs. and Sat. out Mon. Wed. and Frid
  John Giddens.
London, in Mon. and Tues out Tues. and Frid John Webb.
Shepton Mallet, in Tues. and Frid. out Wed. and Sat. Ditto.
Trowbridge, in and out Tues and Frid. R. Gadley.
Coleford and Halcomb, in Frid. out Sat. John Gane.

BELL, Thomas-ftreet. (John Lee)
Bath, in and out every day. Anna Bafcum.
Exeter, Taunton, Wellington and Cullumpton, in Tues. and
  Thurs. out Wed. and Frid. James Parfons.
Devizes, in and out Tues. and Sat. William Fifher.
Sherborne, Dorchefter and Weymouth, in Tues. out Wed.
  John Beale.
North-Petherton, and North-Curry, in Thurs. out Frid. Birt
  and Tirtlet.
Worle, Wefton, &c. in and out every Sat. George Young.

SWAN, Maryport-ftreet. (A. Cuddeford)
Tetbury, Stroud, &c. in and out every Wed. Richard Haven.
Sodbury, in and out Mon. Wed and Sat. Robert Adlam.
Wotton-under Edge, in Tues. and Frid. out Wed. and Sat.
  Samuel Peglar.
Frenchay, Frampton and Winterbourne, in and out every day.
  John New.
Berkley, and places adjacent, in Tues. out Wed. Edw. Clark.
Thornbury, Tues. and Frid. —— Allen.
Durfley, Cam, and places adjacent, in Mon. and Tues. out Thurs.
  and Frid Daniel Loungftreeth.

LAMB, Broad-mead. (John Anderfon)
Thornbury, in and out Wed. and Sat. —— Roberts.
Tetbury, in Tues. and Frid. out Wed and Sat. Wm. Price.
Uley, and parts adjacent, in Mon. out Tues Charles Ferebee.
Wotton-under Edge, in Tues. and Frid. out Wed. and Sat. J.
  Bennet.

N

LAMB,

LAMB, West-street. (Mary Bartlett)

Marlborough and Newbery, in Tues. and Frid. out Wed. and Thurs. ——— Potter.

Oxford, in Wed. out Thurs. Anthony Jewkes.

Calne, twice a week, (days uncertain) ——— Lewis.

Chippenham, twice a week, (days uncertain) ——— Dallin.

COASTERS to and from BRISTOL.

IRISH TRADERS.——Constant.

Cork. Hibernia, Hall; Penelope, Barry; Elizabeth, Copplestone; Lady Fitzgerrald, Crosby; Adventure, Knight; Providence, Blackford; Prince of Wales, Watkins; Sophia, Weeks.

Dublin. Flora, Hodgson; Warren, Hodgson; Mary, Jones, Draper, Gardener; Bristol, Churnside.

Waterford. Thomas and Mary, Casey; Helen, Keefe; Happy Return, Redmond.

☞ For freight, &c. apply to *D. Fisher*, Broker, Quay

CONSTANT COASTERS.

Aberthaw. Barry Castle, Biss; Sprightly, Banks; in and out every Spring; at the 1st Ladder, Bristol Back.

Barnstaple. Active, Day; Dispatch, Eastway; Liberty, Wittrow Sprightly, Leworthy; Some of these in and out every spring 1st Slip, below the Drawbridge, on the Quay.

Biddeford. Thomas, Heay; Polly, May; in and out every spring; same Slip.

Boscastle. Sally, Moyes; Elizabeth, Bond; in and out every month; same Slip.

Bude. Blessing, Bond; Peggy, Burrows; in and out every spring same Slip.

Cardigan. Speedwell, Davis; 4th Slip, Bristol Back.

Cardiff. Cardiff Castle, Walters; Friends, Evans; Lady Cardiff, Jones; Venus, Jeffries; in and out every spring; 2d Ladder, Bristol Back.

Caermarthen. Caermarthen Packet, Phillips; Emlyn, Mills Speedwell, Jones; Providence, James; Constant Trader, Sheppard; Mayflower, Meredith. Some of these in and out every week. 1st Slip, Bristol Back.

Chester. Nancy, Morris; Peter, Jones; ———, Butterfield in and out every month. Little Slip, at the Quay.

Dartmouth and Exeter. Royal George, Owen; in and out once a month. Same Slip. Falmouth

Falmouth. Hopewell, Rosewell; Industry, Stevens; Sisters, Nash; Speedwell, Dennis; some of these in and out every spring. Dial Slip, at the Quay.

Fowey. Friendship, Davis; the Sisters, and the Bacchus, Butterfield; in and out once a month. Broad Slip, at the Quay.

Greenock. Sisters, Law; uncertain. Near the Drawbridge, Quay.

Hartland. Recovery, Saunders; each of the Bristol Fairs, other times uncertain. 1st Slip, below the Drawbridge, Quay.

Lancaster. Hannah, Mofs; uncertain Little Slip, Quay.

Liverpool. Bristol, Pruft; Liverpool, Jofe; Mayflower, Yeo; some in and out every month. Crane No. 1, Quay.

London. Daniel, Powell; Chard, Honywell; Partridge, Burrowdale, Pollard, Farquharfon; Mervin, Jarman; some of these in and out every month. Cranes, No. 3 and 4, Quay.

Laugharn. Hazard, Allen; Rodney, Davis; in and out once a month. 1st Slip, Bristol Back.

Milford and Haverfordweft. Milford, Crunn; Haverfordweft, Jackfon; Liberty, Whittow; some of these in and out every spring. Same Slip.

Minehead. Unity, Atwill; Nancy, Jenkins; in and out every spring. 5th Slip, Bristol Back.

Neath. Neath Trader, Walters; in and out once a month, 4th Slip, Bristol Back.

Newton. Nancy and Speedy, Lewis; in and out once a month. 1st Ladder, Bristol Back.

Padstow. Patfey, Peters; John and Mary, Vivan; Friendship, Richards, in and out once a month. Broad Slip, Quay.

Pembroke. Sufannah, Jenkins; in and out once a month. 1st Slip, Bristol Back.

Penzance. Friends Goodwill, Clark; Three Brothers, Widge; in and out once a month. Broad Slip, Quay.

Plymouth. Rover, Lowman; Dove, Cooper; Unity, Cooper; Hope, Pynfent; Lamb, Hall; Jacob, Hewetfon; some in and out every spring. Broad and Dial Slips, Quay.

Poole, Portfmouth, and Southampton. Cams Delight, Oliver, Elizabeth, Morris; in and out once a month. Broad Slip, Quay.

Porlock. Two Sisters, Perkins; Fanny, Moore, each Bristol Fairs, other times uncertain. 6th Slip, Bristol Back.

St. Ives and Hayle. John and Betfy, Cundy; Hayle Trader, Cundy; Bristol Trader, Rowe, in and out once a month. Broad Slip, Quay.

Swanfea. Sisters, Nichols; Phœnix, Dimond; in and out every spring. 4th Slip, Bristol Back.

Tenby. Blefling, Wickland; Endeavour, Griffith; in and out

once

once a month. 1st Ladder, Briftol Back.

Watchet. Friends Increafe, Jenkins; Profper, Jenkins; Social Friends, Hole; in and out every fpring. 5th Ship, Briftol Back.

SEVERN TROWS.

In and out every Spring....Head of the Quay.

Bewdly. Hopewell, Steward; Induftry, Taylor; Hopewell, Tyler; John, Edwards.——Carries to Stourport and all places in the North.

Bridgnorth. Neptune, Beard; Brittania, Bufh.

Frampton. Friendfhip, Hopkins

Glocefter. Betty, Wakefield; John, Wakefield; Jane, Jones; carries to Glocefter, Salop, &c.

Newnham. Friendfhip, Adams.

Stroud. Stroud Galley, Gaifbrook; carries to Stroud, Oxford and London.

Tewkefbury. Edward, Miller; carries to Tewkefbury, Evefham, and all places in the North.

Upton. Charlotte, Ricketts; Molly, Pomfrey; carries to Upton, Ledbury, &c.

Worcefter. Ark, Baffet; Neptune, Beard; Profper, Radford, Endeavour, Gardner; Molly, Pugh; Sifters, Pearce; carries to Worcefter, Stourport, and all places in the North.

WYE TROWS, in and out every Spring,
Market-houfes, Briftol Back.

Abbey Tintern and Brockwar. The Abbey, Maxley; Wilton, Pritchard; Antelope, Morris.

Hereford. Hereford, and John and Mary, Sinar;

Monmouth. Endeavour, Hughes; Monmouth, Dibden.

MARKET BOATS, in and out every Week.

Caerleon. The Caerleon Boat, Gethin; in Wed. out Thurf. 2d Slip, Briftol Back.

Chepftow. The Chepftow Boat, Jane; in Wed out Thurf. Same Slip.

Newport. The Moderator, Jones; in Wed. out Thurf. Same Slip.
———— The Tredegar, Waters; in Wed. out Thurf. Same Slip.

☞ Barges for conveyance of goods to and from *Bath* twice a week conftantly. ..*Market-Houfe,* on the *Back, Bath Barge,* and *Queen's-Head, Queen-ftreet.*

DIRECTIONS

DIRECTIONS *for Travellers, &c. when to pass the* SEVERN *between* ENGLAND *and* WALES.

At Auft (or the Old Paffage) it is about two miles over to Beachley, in the parifh of Tidenham, Gloceftershire. This is the direct way to Newent, Newnham, and all the Foreft of Dean, Herefordfhire, Worcefterfhire, and the upper part of Monmouth-fhire.

At the New Paffage, it is about three miles over at high water to Port Skewith, near St. Pierre, in Monmouthfhire. This is the direct way to Cardiff, Caerleon, Fontypool, and moft parts of South Wales.

As the croffing at either of the above Paffages depends on the winds, it is neceffary to obferve, that they diftinguifh but two winds for paffing, viz winds below, and winds above.

Winds below, are when it blows up the river Southerly or Wefterly. With thefe you may pafs during the ebb or going out of the tide, which is 7 hours.

Winds above, are when it blows down the river Northerly or Eafterly. with thefe there is 5 hours paffing, on the flood or coming in of the tide. When the wind is S. E. or N. W. it is directly acrofs the river, therefore you muft be at the Paffage where you intend to crofs, an hour before high water.

The difference of paffing at Auft and the New Paffage, varies about an hour; tide coming in, wind above, New Paffage is an hour fooner than Auft, tide going out, wind below, Auft is an hour fooner than New,

Prices of Paffage.

A four wheel carriage 10s. Two wheel ditto 5s. Man and Horfe 1s. Horfe alone 8d. Foot paffenger 6d. Cattle per head 6d. Sheep or pigs per fcore 2s. 6d.

N. B. A fmall boat hired on purpofe to crofs over is 5s. exclufive of paffage.

HOLIDAYS obferved at the CUSTOM-HOUSE.

January 1, 6, 18, 25, 30*.	July 25.
February 2, 24.	Auguft 1*, 12*, 24.
March 25	September 21, 22*, 29.
April 23, 25.	October 18, 25, 26*, 28.
May 1, 19*, 29*.	November 1, 4, 5*, 30,
June 4*, 11, 24, 29.	December 21, 25, 26, 27, 28.

Those days marked thus * if they happen on a Sunday are kept on Monday.

Besides which, the under-mentioned HOLIDAYS are kept on the Days they respectively happen.

Ash Wednesday—Good Friday—Monday Tuesday, and Wednesday in Easter Week—Holy Thursday—Monday, Tuesday, and Wednesday in Whitsun-Week.

ERRATA.

Page 73, line 32, for Limekiln-lane, read Lower College-st.
Page 78, line 1, for James, read Thomas.
Page 82, line 15, for Hotwell-parade, read Paradise-row.

Clergy.—Brickendon, Rev. R. St. Vincents-parade.
Spencer, Rev. T. Jacobs-well.
Dissent. Clergy.—Jacomb, Rev. Mr. Brunswick-square.
Ryland, Rev. J. North-street.
Physic.—Davies, David, *Surgeon*, Park-street.
Hale, John, *Surgeon*, College-street.
Renaudet,   *M. D.* Hotwell-parade.
Traders.—Andrass, John, *Turner*, Wine-street.
Andrass, Jane, *Milliner*,   Ditto.
Baugh, Francis, *Basket-maker*, Redcliff-street.
Begg, James, *Mason*, Upper Maudlin-lane.
Broderip, Robert, *Musician*, Kingsdown.
Bruce, Robert, *Merchant*, 15, Orchard-street.
Chabas, John, *Fencing-master*, over the Market-house, H.g.d.
Chapman, James, *Architect*, Milk-street.
Chilcott, Thomas, *Linen-draper*, Wine-street.
Cloud, John, *Roap and Twine-maker*, Bedminster.
Coleman, B. Freeman, 1, King-square.
Cook, Robert, *Portrait-painter*, Queen-square.
Crawfoord, Baker, and Co. *Cheese-factors*, Redcliff-street.
Culliford and Thomas, *Wine-merchants*, Broad-street.
Fenley, John, *Bookbinder*, &c. Broad-mead.
Fergusson, Robert, Esq. 7, Queens-parade.
Fox, Charles, *Miniature-painter*, Alfred-place.
Fox, Charles, Gent. Brunswick-square.
Garmston, Paul, *Bright-smith*, Bread-street.
Greeniv, Edward, Esq. Rodney-place, Clifton.
Hancock,   *Ladies' Hair-dresser*, Clifton-hill.
Hatheway, John, *Mathematical Academy*, Montague-street
Hazell, Thomas, *Leather-dresser*, Back-hall.
Henson and Parsons, *Cabinet-makers*, Broad Ware.
Houghton, Peter, *Leather-seller*, Bridewell-lane.
Howell, John, *Cabinet-maker*, Redcliff-street.   Hughes

Hughes, John, *Carpenter*, Clifton-hill.
Johnston, George Milligen, Efq. *M. D.* College-green. **Does** not practice.
Joy, Philip, *Shroud-maker*, St. Johns-fteps.
King, Thomas, *Bookseller*, Quay-street.
Lewis, John, *Taylor*, Old-market.
Locker, William, *Spring Gardens*, Hotwell-road.
Mills, Susannah, *Grocer*, Milk-street.
Morgan, Morgan, *Mason and Builder*, Newfoundland-street.
Morgan, John, *Coach and Horses*, Grove.
Narraway, John, *Leather-dreffer*, Broad-mead.
Owen, Mary, *Laundrefs*, Hotwells.
Pearfe, John, *Mason*, Charlotte-street, St. Pauls.
Perry, William, *Broker*, Corn-street.
Poflon, George, *White Hart Inn*, Broad-street.
Pownall, S. *Dealer in Horses*, Limekiln-lane.
Purnell, John, *Mufician*, Clifton-hill.
Radford, John, *Chandler*, St. Michaels-hill.
Riddle, Richard, *Crown and Anchor*, Kill-kenny.
Salway, George, *Hair-dreffer*, Broad-street.
Savyer, Charles, *Writing-mafter*, Kingfdown.
Slade and Barratt, *Grocers*, Redcliff-hill.
Smith, Robert, Efq. Princes-place, Clifton.
Stewart, Archibald, Gent. Pembroke-court.
Symes, Richard, *Merchant*, Colftons-parade.
Toutle, Richard, *Tyler and Plaifterer*, Unity-street, St. Philips.
Vanderhorft, Davis, and Co. *Merchants*, Small-street.
Wagner, I M. *Merchant*, Broad-street.
Wenfley and Collins, *Linen-drapers*, High-street.
Williams, J. and T. *Malt-mill makers*, Tower-hill
Wilmot, Edward Coke, 8, St. James's-fquare.
Winter, George, *Wine-merchant*, Orchard-street.
Woolefon, Mrs. Hefter, St. James's church-yard.

F I N I S.